STEEL ON THE BOTTOM

GREAT LAKES SHIPWRECKS

FREDERICK STONEHOUSE

D1479129

Avery Color Studios, Inc.
Gwinn, Michigan

© 2006 Avery Color Studios, Inc.

ISBN-13: 978-1-892384-35-5
ISBN-10: 1-892384-35-3

Library of Congress Control Number: 2005935594

First Edition–2006

10   9   8   7   6   5

Published by Avery Color Studios, Inc.
Gwinn, Michigan 49841

Cover photo: Stonehouse Collection, back cover
photo: Ric Mixter

✳ TABLE OF CONTENTS ✳

✳ Introduction ✳

A while back the thought occurred to me I hadn't written a pure shipwreck book in a very long time, in fact ten years! In the interval I wrote books on the US Life-Saving Service, Great Lakes maritime ghosts, Great Lakes maritime crime, a couple of kids books and even a cookbook. It clearly was time to do another shipwreck book. And thus was born *Steel On The Bottom*.

I didn't want to make it a geographically limited book, not a "shipwrecks of" kind of thing. Nor did I want to really tie them together with a tight common theme, all schooners wrecks or wrecks after 18-something.

After due reflection, I decided I would just write about steel wrecks I found interesting, without regard to time, geography or common theme beyond steel construction. In large measure I guess I am the only common thread.

I hope you will find it interesting.

Please note that my chart locations are only for general orientation and not intended to be precise.

PERE MARQUETTE 18

"The boat's all right; we'll save her."
September 9, 1910

One of the great unsolved mysteries of Lake Michigan is the *Pere Marquette 18 (PM)*, lost on September 9, 1910. It is a story filled with drama, controversy and wild theory. There are more twists and turns than a Milwaukee pretzel. And there are no real answers.

The Pere Marquette Railroad operated the largest car ferry operation on Lake Michigan. The company was formed from three different lines; the Flint and Pere Marquette (FPM), Chicago and West Michigan and Detroit, Grand Rapids and Western. Ludington, Michigan became the terminus of the operation in 1874 when the FPM first chartered a freighter to haul goods across the lake. The first fleet built car ferry, the *Pere Marquette*, was in service in 1897. It was more efficient to carry the traffic across the lake than run it around the barrier of Lake Michigan. Other ships soon followed as traffic increased.[i]

The *Pere Marquette 18*, usually just called the *PM 18*, was built by the American Shipbuilding Company in Cleveland, Ohio. She was 338 feet in length, had a 58-foot beam and 20.5-foot depth. To facilitate her role as a

PM18 was the pride of the line. Stonehouse Collection

car ferry, four sets of railroad tracks capable of holding a total of 30 rail cars were laid into the lower deck. She had 50 cabins and additional berths for passengers. As the flagship, she had the best cabin appointments of the entire fleet. A superbly furnished day cabin ran the entire length of the ship to assure room and comfort for her passengers.[ii] Twin steam engines gave her enough power to drive along at 22 knots, very fast for such a large vessel. She had a schedule to keep and speed was important. Although crew size varied based on needs, a typical number was 61.

Her design was highly thought of as proved by the construction of the car ferry *Manistique, Marquette And Northern No. 1* for the Manistique, Marquette and Northern Railroad in 1904. A second vessel was planned but never ordered.[iii]

Rail tracks were laid directly onto the carferry deck. This photo is of the City of Milwaukee. *Stonehouse Collection*

The new *PM 18* was sponsored by Beatrice Logan, the daughter of the ship's designer. Ominously instead of breaking the customary bottle of booze on her bow, the owners followed the Japanese custom of releasing doves as she slid down into the water. Doubtless old timers just shook their heads at such an insult to the lake gods. Birds may be fine for the Emperor of Japan, but certainly not for America. Events proved the purists correct. There was only one proper way to christen a ship and it meant a breaking a bottle of hooch on the bow and had nothing to do with foul polluting birds![iv]

The *PM 18* usually ran from Ludington, Michigan to Milwaukee with occasional trips to Manitowoc as traffic dictated. Typical cargos westward included, lumber, chemicals, farm machinery and fruit. Coming back the cars were loaded with Wisconsin favorites such as cheese and beer as well as industrial machinery. Whatever the railroads hauled, so hauled the *PM 18*.

Generally the ferries ran all winter. Commerce didn't stop because the water became "hard." The *PM 18's* powerful engines were not provided just for speed but also so she could punch her way through ice as needed. However, sometimes she did get stuck, hung up in more ice than even she could batter through.

On February 13 the *PM* became wedged in the hard white stuff off Kewaunee, Wisconsin. *PM 18* was sent to her rescue and after locating her, went to work trying to break her out. Although she managed to free her on the 14th both ships were caught fast again five miles west of Manitowoc. It took two days to smash free but not without damage. The *PM 18* broke three of four blades off a screw when a log got caught in it. When more help

PM18 *in drydock having work done on her port shaft.*
Stonehouse Collection

was needed *PM 17* came out and broke both ships free of
the grasping ice. All three suffered some level of hull
damage.[v] Steel was always stronger than ice but there
was one hell of a lot of ice!

After repairs the *PM 18* was back breaking a path
through the ice from Ludington to Manitowoc when she
became stuck and the following *PM* couldn't stop in
time, smashing into her stern, damaging the *PM 18's* car
deck. Sending two ferries together was common in the
winter. The more powerful one ran ahead, breaking a path
for the second. One was headed for the Chicago and
Northwestern dock and the other for the Wisconsin
Central slip. Sending two together also meant there was
help available if one became jammed in the ice.[vi]

Life continued along the expected routine for *PM 18*, shuttling rail cars and passengers across the lake and back as traffic required. In March 1907 an opportunity opened to generate unexpected revenue. The owners of the passenger steamer *Eastland*, which ran out of Chicago as an excursion boat, decided to relocate her to Cleveland. They expected a better opportunity for excursion trips on Lake Erie.[vii] The *Eastland* already had a reputation as a "tender" ship and knowledgeable sailors claimed she was unsafe and someday would capsize with horrendous results. Doubtless no one forecast the terrible events of July 1914, when she rolled at her Chicago River berth, killing an estimated 844 people. It was the worst maritime disaster on the Great Lakes.

The steamer Eastland's *transfer to Cleveland opened the way for the* PM-18's *conversion to a summer excursion steamer. Stonehouse Collection*

The *Eastland* departure got the "wheels turning" and some real "out of the box" thinking occurred. Before long the Chicago and South Haven Steamship Company made a deal with the railroad to charter the *PM 18* for the summer, bringing her to Chicago for use as an excursion steamer. Given the other vessels in the fleet, *PM 15, 17* and *19* could carry the summer traffic. It was a good opportunity to earn some unexpected revenue. Chartering her out during the summer made a lot of economic sense. The *PM 18* had the largest passenger capacity of the fleet, plus the freight business was slower in the summer than winter. Whether it was a straight charter for cash, or the railroad would receive a cut of the tickets sold, isn't known. The local paper considered the opportunity to be very worthwhile stating, "The proposition to convert the huge steel car ferry into a popular short run excursion boat for Chicago people is at once original, big and unique. Yet everybody who knows the boat says the scheme is a winner." It further stated "the Lake Michigan Excursion Company (authors note, the company chartering the *PM 18*) must keep up the insurance on the boat and return her at the end of two months in as good condition as when she was chartered." The paper estimated the expense of fitting her out for the cruise business at $10,000 to $15,000, a considerable sum for a short 60 day season. But with the *PM 18* carrying up to 5,000 passengers at a time and two trips a day, it could be very profitable.[viii]

Further details of the plan slowly emerged. The charter company billed the *PM 18* as the "world's greatest excursion steamer," and marketed her as a unique novelty to Chicago. Before going to Chicago a crew of workers

Thousands of excursionists lined PM18's *decks.*
Stonehouse Collection

covered the main and car decks with wooden floors, built two large stairways aft and cut gangways for entrances in both sides among other alterations. The lower car deck, normally filled with rail cars was the scene of amusements including dancing pavilions, palm gardens, music and slot machines and games. Both a band and orchestra were planned for as well as a steam calliope. Just to be on the safe side, 5,000 life jackets were also placed aboard. Daily runs to Waukegan were planned for five days a week, departing at 9:00 a.m. and returning at 4:00 p.m., followed by moonlight excursions around Chicago. Saturday was devoted to local excursions and on Sunday she ran to South Haven for the day.

Ominously the *PM 18* would be in constant motion without a moment of rest or maintenance.[ix]

The charter operator promoted the excursions heavily, the Ludington paper claiming $25,000 was spent on the effort, including posters, newspaper ads and billboards.[x]

The new excursion boat proved a quick success. On July 4th she carried 4,862 people from Chicago to South Haven, nearly 98 percent of capacity. She was a genuine novelty to Chicagoans and they, "are flocking in thousands to see and ride on the famous craft. A moonlight excursion on Lake Michigan is given every night and these events in good weather are patronized by thousands of people. On the main deck 5,000 square feet of floor space are reserved for dancing and 10,000 for palm gardens. On the boat there are free vaudeville and orchestra attractions day and night."[xi] Thousands of people enjoyed the cool refreshing lake breezes while cruising on the big floating amusement park.

If there was a fly in the ointment it was the master, Captain Peter Kilty. In early July he gave up command and returned to Ludington suffering from a bout of rheumatism. It was initially claimed he would "take the baths" for a time then return to duty with another ship. Captain William LaFlour of *PM 19* replaced him on the *18*. Kilty was expected to return to the *18* when she returned from the Chicago charter in early September.[xii]

PM 18 returned to Ludington on September 3, her charter declared by all to have been a rousing success. The decking, stairways and related fixtures were quickly removed and stored for another year with the clear expectation of a subsequent charter. The *PM 18* was again soon running cars.[xiii]

———————

Throughout the fall and winter the *PM 18* fell back into the regular routine of a Lake Michigan car ferry. Load'em up and haul'em over, then back again, fair weather or foul, soft water or hard ice, it was all part of the trade.

The Chicago excursion contract was renewed for the 1908 season. From all accounts it too was a successful season, the *PM 18* hauling thousands of excursionists in safety and comfort. A ticket for the run to Waukegan was 25 cents with the same for a "moonlight" cruise around Chicago on the, "Leviathan of the Inland Seas," with departures from the Wells Street Bridge.[xiv] When she returned to Ludington at the end of the season the local paper bragged, "All summer long *No. 18* has been nothing more nor less than a mammoth floating amusement garden, a palace of splendid architecture, a summer resort which has conveyed its patrons over miles of dancing waters." When she reached her docks the finery was stripped away and she received two weeks of hurried maintenance before starting another season of winter sailing.[xv]

The winter was a tough one for the fleet. Storms and ice bedeviled the ferries all season. *PM 17* went up on a sand bar north of Ludington in a storm and was only recovered with difficulty. Saving her from loss was a near thing. Regardless of the difficulties, *PM 18* apparently kept her schedule, driving into foaming, ice choked Lake Michigan without respite, day in and day out.

For nine weeks during the summer of 1909 *PM 18* was back to being a Chicago excursion steamer, now for the newly organized Chicago Navigation Company. It was claimed she only missed three trips due to weather all

PM 18 *pounding through the ice entering Ludington. Stonehouse Collection*

summer, a remarkable record. As in prior years, Captain J. C. Ackerman was her master. Newspapers proudly bellowed she carried over 500,000 summer passengers! As in previous years she was to receive a quick refit before going into winter railroad service.[xvi]

The summer of 1910 was not successful. The crowds were light and the promoters lost money. Apparently the bloom was off the rose and the big steamer was no longer the attraction of days past. The decision was made not to use *PM 18* as a summer cruiser again. Before she left Chicago for Ludington all of her special fitting and decoration were removed and sold. There would be no more moonlight cruises with thousands of happy people enjoying the gentle zephyrs of Lake Michigan.[xvii]

After *PM 18* was lost, the claim was made that the summer trips, "wore her out, that the hull and engines were damaged. She was an eggshell ready to crack at the slightest injury." It was alleged she was badly handled at docks, with the boat striking the pilings at Chicago hard enough to break them off injuring her hull plates.[xviii]

A short piece in the *Ludington Chronicle* for September 7, 1910 implied Captain Kilty, the winter master, was stunned by the shape *PM 18* ship was in when she returned from Chicago. Reputedly he cried, "What have they done to my ship?" *PM 18* was leaking enough to require her pumps to run continuously and when he punched the hull with his elbow to test the strength of the plate, he claimed it was a weak as an eggshell. Plates were loose and rattled when the engines were running and he wanted her sent to the yard for extensive repair.[xix]

———————

Newspapers later claimed he told his wife before the first ferry run she would never make it to Milwaukee except for a miracle. He said the ferry was doomed! Although he tried to have the Pere Marquette superintendent hold her back for repair, his appeals were ignored.ˣˣ

Regardless of his fears, Captain Peter Kilty departed with *PM 18* at 11:30 p.m., Thursday, September 8, with a full load of 29 railcars of coal and general merchandise secured on the car deck. There was some speculation later that he hurried a bit to avoid leaving on a Friday, a notorious bad luck day for starting a season. If so, this was just following an old maritime tradition. There was a strong north wind and heavy sea on the lake but otherwise the weather was good. Sixty-one souls were aboard her.ˣˣⁱ

Kilty was born on Beaver Island in 1860. His family fished out of St. James Harbor on the island's north east point and he learned the lake trade from his earliest days. Beaver Island is about 20 miles or so northwest from Charlevoix, Michigan and at the time was the center of a very rich commercial fishing business. He later fished a small schooner out of Onekema, a miniscule village just north of Manistee, Michigan and later captained a local fish tug. But bigger things beckoned for this Beaver Island sailor. He soon took a job with the Northern Michigan Line running from Chicago and later shifted to the *Ann Arbor No. 1* car ferry in 1896. She was his first car ferry and he never sailed another type of vessel. Two years later he started as a master with the Pere Marquette Train Ferry Company. Respected in the community, he was well known as a gentleman with a serious bent. It was claimed he never got more than two hours of sleep on any trip and rarely was he not in the pilothouse when the ship was on the open lake. He left a wife, two sons and a daughter behind when he perished in the wreck.[xxii]

Joseph Brezinski was the first mate. His younger brother Frank was an engineer on *PM 17*. Originally his family planned to accompany him to Milwaukee, but changed their minds at the last minute and were spared the violence of the wreck.

Peter Kilty of PM 18.
Stonehouse Collection

All went well until about 4:30 a.m. when the Captain was told the ship was flooding aft. Considering the pumps were already running when she left Ludington, they couldn't handle the additional water. The vessel was about halfway across the Lake, over five hours from Milwaukee, so turning back made no sense.

There are different versions to events surrounding the flooding. Supposedly an oiler went down through the flicker to oil some bearings on the propeller shafts and he discovered seven feet of water in the aft compartment. He reported it back to the engineer who in turn notified the pilothouse with the result the first mate came down to inspect. He identified the water as coming from an open deadlight, which quickly closed. But the water continued to gush in from somewhere else. As the stern settled deeper, several deadlights now below the surface broke and more water streamed into the ship. To balance out the now lower stern, water was counter flooded into a forward compartment.[xxiii]

Surviving crewman James Koob positively claimed however he closed all the deadlights before leaving Ludington. Wherever the water came from, it wasn't his deadlights.[xxiv]

Kilty brought his officers together and quickly decided to change course for Sheboygan. It was 50 miles closer than Milwaukee and given his present situation, every mile meant better odds of getting to a safe harbor or even running her on the beach. The Captain is remembered as being very cool and collected, assessing the situation and giving orders as needed.

Immediately Kilty ordered the crew to start dumping railcars in an effort to lighten ship. First mate Joe Brezinski took charge and in quick order, chains were dropped from the belaying rings and nine cars were laboriously and slowly pushed over the stern.[xxv] Some survivors claimed it increased freeboard by two feet. Others said it did little good. It was a temporary respite at best. Water continued to flood in. Pushing the cars off was also very difficult. When an attempt was made to shove the first one off it hung up, resting on the forward trucks and then the middle of the car. The crew used hand rams to force it inch by inch until it finally toppled over. There was no locomotive on board so the only power was muscle and a few small hydraulic rams. When they finished with the cars, the men laid out a towing hawser in the expectation *PM 17* would need it to bring them in to port in the event the engine room flooded.[xxvi]

———————

The crew kept their spirits up throughout the day. When they finished pushing cars off, the deckhands retreated to the galley for sandwiches and coffee. Some men sang and others just talked. All joked about how close they came to sinking. Many were stripped to their shirts and sweating from the heavy exertion with the cars.

About ten minutes before she sank, Chief Engineer Ross Leedham spoke with Kilty about the situation. Since the engine room wasn't yet flooded and Leedham still able to deliver full power *PM 18* pounded on for shore with the pumps running at maximum. The pair finished talking and the engineer went back below, closing the hatch behind him. When *PM 18* dove for the bottom the closed hatch likely kept the engine room gang from escaping their steel walled tomb.

At 5:00 a.m. Kilty instructed the wireless operator, 22-year-old Stephen F. Sczepanek, to send out an SOS. "Car ferry *18* is sinking midlake - help - answer - answer," went crackling out over the airwaves. At 5:20 a.m. another frantic message was sent. "C Q D - C Q D - the water got over stern." Twenty minutes later Sczepanek tapped out, "*17 - 17 - 17 - 18 -* come help - come help - *17 - 17 - 19*." Unfortunately the set on *PM 18* only

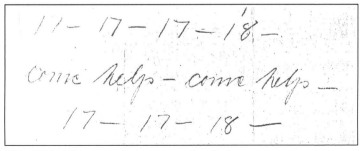

The PM-18's *cryptic message for help. Stonehouse Collection*

transmitted. It did not receive messages. *PM 17* was off Port Washington, Wisconsin heading back to Ludington and responded quickly to the call. Captain Joseph Russell found *PM 18* about 20 miles off Sheboygan at 7:00 a.m. It was apparent to him she was in deep trouble, low in the water and the national ensign at half-mast.[xxvii]

The Pere Marquette Railroad adopted wireless earlier on, considering it far superior than using homing pigeons for communication. Prior to radio, pigeons were the accepted standard for ship to shore messages.[xxviii]

Sczepanek, a native of Worcester, Massachusetts, had prior experience with making distress calls. On January 7, 1910 he tapped out a call for the Goodrich steamer *Arizona* on Lake Michigan. She was about three hours out of Chicago on the run to Grand Haven and Muskegon when her cylinder head blew, resulting in the vessel filling with thick smoke. Everyone presumed fire and panicked, especially when the source couldn't be readily found. However, Sczapanek kept his head and used his radio to call the head office in Chicago and sister ships *Indiana* and *Iowa* resulting in the ship being safely towed back to Chicago. Like most operators of the time he was employed by a radio company, in this case the

Captain Joseph Russell of PM 17. *Stonehouse Collection*

United Wireless Company, not PM and was onboard as a contract employee only.[xxix]

Sczepanek was the first wireless operator to die in service on the Great Lakes. In recognition, his name is listed on a memorial in New York City just below that of Jack Phillips, the wireless operator who perished on the *Titanic* in April 1912. Known as the "Jack Phillips Titanic Memorial Fountain," it was located at the base of the U.S. State Barge Office. In the center of the fountain was an eight-foot high cenotaph with the names of heroic wireless operators who lost their lives, "in the line of duty." The $3,000 used to erect the memorial was raised by contributions from wireless operators on Atlantic and coastwise duty and Great Lakes. When dedicated in 1915 eight names were inscribed and more have been added. The memorial still exists at Battery Park at the foot of Manhattan facing the inner harbor and Statue of Liberty although the fountain is gone.[xxx]

Sczepanek's name is on the Jack Phillips Titanic Memorial Fountain in New York City.
Stonehouse Collection

Kilty told *PM 17's* Russell to standby. He was going to keep heading for Sheboygan but if sinking seemed imminent, he wanted

PM 17 *came to the rescue but it was too late.*
Stonehouse Collection

him close. As a precaution, Kilty also had all of the port side lifeboats lowered although he didn't order the crew and passengers into life jackets. For reasons that are still unclear, perhaps Russell told him to send it, or he assumed too much, the radio operator on *PM 17* sent a message to the Pere Marquette office in Ludington that everyone on *PM 18* was safe. This erroneous message created great confusion and heartbreak among family members.

The wind was still blowing hard and the lake was rough, but it wasn't truly stormy. The conditions were typical for commercial steamers on the Lakes and certainly nothing *PM 18* should have any concern about.

At about 7:35 a.m. *PM 18* could no longer keep afloat. The crew on the *PM 17* was horrified to unexpectedly see her stern settle suddenly into the water and bow rise high in the sky, propelling her to the bottom, stern first! It

A postcard depicting the sinking of PM18.
Stonehouse Collection

happened so quickly, there was no time to use the lifeboats. Passengers and crew on the *PM 18* were caught totally unaware. As she sank air pressure blew out cabin roofs, windows and the stacks, witnesses claiming people flew 30 feet into the air! Her boilers may have blown too when the cold water touched them but this is speculation. The spot of lake where the ferry had been just moments before was a mass of floating wreckage interspersed with occasional survivors clinging to whatever floating debris they could find. Reports differ as to where Captain Kilty was located when she plunged to the bottom. Some witnesses said he was on the flying bridge; others that he was amidships on the main deck. Regardless of location, he perished with his ship.

The crew aboard *PM 17* immediately launched lifeboats to go to the aid of the survivors. The first boat was caught by the waves and smashed against the hull, killing mates Joseph Peterson and Robert Jacobson. Two

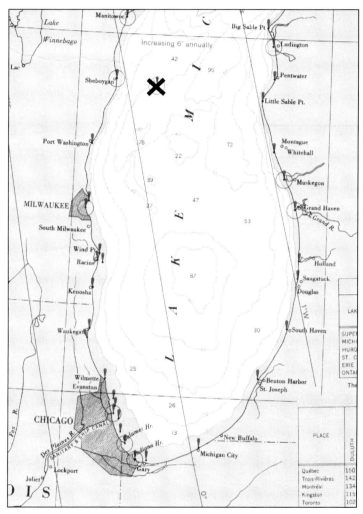

other men in the boat were injured but rescued. The
second boat was launched without problems and in less
than an hour it managed to pull 14 survivors aboard. A
third lifeboat saved another 13 people. As quickly as they
were hauled aboard *PM 17* the survivors were wrapped in
heavy blankets, given stimulants and put to bed. Many

went immediately to sleep remaining so until the ferry reached Ludington.[xxxi]

Additional rescuers also soon arrived on the scene. *PM 20* and *PM 6* and the Port Washington tug *A.A. Tessler* accounted for another six survivors making a total of 33.[xxxii] Both *PM 20* and *PM 6* were late in departing from Ludington for the wreck because the ferry office considered the distress calls fake. "C Q D" sent by *PM 18* was the old distress call. Their attitude was no one used it anymore so the call had to be a hoax. Only the repetitive nature of the calls finally convinced the men they were real.[xxxiii]

A fleet of vessels eventually blanketed the disaster site, including a Revenue Cutter, tug *Peter Reiss* from Sheboygan towing the local U.S. Life-Saving Station crew in their 34-foot lifeboat, steamer *Syndey Neff*, tugs *Meyer*, *Tessler*, *Ewig* and *Welcome* from Milwaukee and even a powered dredge also from Milwaukee. They found no survivors and few victims, only wreckage. It was too late. Four empty life rafts bobbed on the waves, floating free when the *PM 18* sank. A railcar roof, clothing of all kinds including Kilty's black coat with a wallet filled with money and many life rings danced across the cold waves.[xxxiv]

PM 17 stood by the scene hoping more survivors would be located but it was not to be. The *Tessler* managed to fish up six bodies, scant recompense for the scores lost. All were transferred to what the newspapers called a "life-saving cutter," and later taken to *PM 17*. Since there were no "life-saving cutters" most likely this was a Revenue Marine Service vessel.[xxxv] Each victim was slowly hoisted aboard the car ferry using her lifeboat davits. A rope was

———————

tied off around the shoulders and feet and it was "haul away." The six bodies included Kilty, Marian Turner, the cabin maid, Nelse Bertrand, a salesman fitting new carpet in the steamer, Albert Mack, the steward, William Cummings, a ships agent and Stephen Sczepanek, the purser and radio operator. Marian Turner was still grasping a rosary. Turner was 50 years of age and the only woman aboard the ship. Witnesses on the *PM 17* say they saw her running forward and finally reaching the rail as the bow rose and the ship dove for the bottom. Trained as a nurse, a skill that over the years was valuable to sailors and passengers alike, she left an invalid mother in Ludington.[xxxvi]

Carpet salesman Nelse Bertrand jumped into the water with deckhand Andrew Madison moments before the ship sank. Bertrand was killed when part of the pilothouse blew off the sinking steamer and landed directly on top of him, narrowly missing Madison swimming nearby.

Five of the six bodies immediately recovered wore life jackets. A witness later said blood was streaming out of their noses, indicating they had been sucked under by the sinking ship and crushed to death by the depths. The unidentified body of a seventh victim was recovered shortly before the search was called off. Later *PM 20* recovered the remains of cook Johnny Schraufuagl and first mate Joseph Brezinski.[xxxvii]

Meanwhile back in Ludington the company was planning for dealing with the disaster. Before *PM 17* entered the harbor the tug *Schnorbach* met her and transferred doctors Gray and Kirwin aboard. The pair treated the survivors and assured the dead were appropriately cared for. In a mark of respect for the lost,

PM 17's flag flew at half-mast. When she finally moored, the ferry dock area was mobbed by an estimated 2,000 people, many fighting for choice positions upfront. PM officials kept the survivors in cabins permitting no one to board the vessel until W. L. Trump, the PM superintendent and his men questioned them. The exceptions were crewmen Thomas Shields and Mike Petrosky, deemed by the doctors sufficiently injured to be admitted to the Paulina Stearns Hospital. Shields was suffering from internal injuries caused by being hit with a large beam while Petrosky was in a state of complete exhaustion. Both men were from Chicago so the local papers paid little interest to them. *PM 17* crew were also kept from the crowds until the railroad men were able to debrief them. PM concern was clearly to spin survivor statements to the press. Survivors without clothing were eventually taken to a local haberdashery and provided for at company expense. The dead were later removed from the ship in rough wood coffins and taken to a temporary morgue. The first body off was that of Captain Kilty, borne silently by a crew of Life-Savers as fit his position. Once all the dead were finally ashore, a steady stream of people went through the morgue viewing the remains. Doubtless many were not relations looking for loved ones but instead only the morbidly curious. Mrs. Turner's body was placed in a side room for privacy until relatives claimed it.[xxxviii]

The PM superintendent went on the spin offensive stating, "Our car ferries carried over a million cars and this is the first instance in the history of our line we wet a pound of freight. I have interviewed 33 of the survivors and have utterly failed to extract the slightest bit of information as to the real cause of the disaster. The only ones who could have enlightened me went down with their boat. I cannot see where this disaster reveals any fault in car ferry construction. The sinking was due to causes outside of this." As with later Great Lakes shipwrecks, positioning the loss as an Act of God was financially better than admitting fault. If the loss was the result of PM negligence the compensation costs were higher. An act of God was after all an Act of God and no one's fault.[xxxix]

The superintendent didn't explain why the railroad delayed telling the public *PM 18* was lost. By 7:30 a.m. they were well aware of the tragedy but held back telling anyone until immediate efforts to recover the bodies were finished. Apparently the railroad wanted to at least be able to inform families the remains were in hand and not lost forever in Lake Michigan. By 8:00 a.m. however the secret could no longer be kept and the families were notified. The open radio messages were heard by too many other people to keep the secret.[xl]

Some of the people waiting at the dock were greatly affected, especially those with loved ones on *PM 18*. When *PM 17* signaled all were saved, they were expecting to see their loved one walk off the ship happily waving. To suddenly learn they were dead was a devastating shock. The wives of second mate Walter H. Brown and second assistant engineer Paul Renner were waiting patiently for their husbands to come ashore. When they didn't both women were shattered. Newspapers reported Mrs. Brown was in critical condition from the shock. Second mate Brown, his wife, three-year old boy and their three-week old baby just moved into a new home. The first load of household goods was still unopened.[xli] A highly qualified mariner,

Brown earlier captained the car ferry *Grand Haven* before moving to *PM 18* a short time before. Renner left not only a mourning wife but also a five-week old son.[xlii]

One of the hardest hit was a crewmember who didn't make the trip, Michael Petrosky. When he learned of the sinking he mentally collapsed, displaying such marked evidence of insanity he was locked in jail. While waiting transport to the U.S. Marine Hospital for the Insane in Washington, D.C. he escaped his guards and fled. The demented sailor was finally found walking the lonely beach, looking out into the rolling lake and "murmuring incoherently about Captain Kilty, his shipmates and *No. 18*."[xliii]

Because only nine of the 29 victims were found, there were more memorial services than funerals. The biggest funeral was for Captain Kilty on September 13 at the early hour of 7:30 a.m. The unusual time was explained by the trains with the next scheduled departure at 9:00 a.m. When the service was finished at St. Simon's Catholic Church there was just enough time for the mourners to arrive at the station with his casket for transport to Manistee and internment. A newspaper described the service as "impressive." "At either side of the alter were huge banks of floral pieces, one being a beautiful rose and green anchor, symbolic of the shipmaster's calling." Pallbearers consisted of maritime men, including survivor Frank Young the chief steward of the line.[xliv]

The number of people lost is still open to speculation. The Ludington paper said 29. Other sources claim 27-29 or even more. The problem is a combination of being uncertain of the passengers and the likelihood of stowaways. It is an unsolved mystery.[xlv]

Captain Peter Kilty's headstone. Stonehouse Collection

Many people proposed building a shrine to the men lost in the disaster but nothing came of it. Life just moved on. After all, nothing would bring the dead back.

Apparently no additional bodies were recovered, the assumption being they were trapped within the hull.

As follows many major wrecks, the weirdos came out in full force. One man from Green Bay proposed a new device he just invented to raise the wreck. Essentially it was a set of four powerful magnets combined with large steel air tanks and two steel arches. The whole shebang was lowered to the wreck, the electro magnets switched on to grip the hull and air pumped into the air tanks. "Presto Gizmo and Alakazam," *PM 18* would rise again to the surface of Lake Michigan. After some newspaper hoopla, it turned out to be nothing but a pipe dream.[xlvi]

All matter of wreckage continued to wash ashore on the western beaches of the lake, much of it fouling and tearing commercial fishing nets. Life-Saving Service patrols along the beaches failed to find a single additional victim. The lake had swallowed them forever.

As is typical in shipwreck, the inevitable note in a bottle was found. In this instance it was in a beer bottle discovered on the beach at 64th Street in Chicago on September 23. The cryptic message simply stated, "We

A Michigan Historical Site marker in Ludington commemorates the loss of PM 18. Stonehouse Collection

died bravely. Tell mother" - Signed, "Jimmy." Authorities had the note checked for authenticity by experts at the University of Chicago who considered it genuine, concluding it was quite possible for it to have washed ashore in the interval since the wreck. However there was a significant problem. There was no one lost named "Jimmy." If the note was legitimate it had to be from a stowaway. It was believed there likely were two aboard.[xlvii]

An article in the *Kalamazoo Gazette* claimed *PM 18* was leaking as the result of striking a dock during her excursion days and opened a seam in her plates. Two local Steamboat Inspectors from Grand Haven, who checked the boat before she left Ludington maintained she was in good shape and undamaged. The paper claimed when she was strained by the waves on the open lake, the seams opened further and down she went.[xlviii]

Family members blamed the railroad. Mrs. Kilty said her husband told her the ship was not seaworthy and he hesitated three times before finally departing. Mrs. Brown, the wife of the second mate, stated her husband and Kilty had bad feelings about the run. Mrs. Leedham, the engineer's widow, said her husband spoke to both men and was told the "ship would be in no suitable condition to go out except for another week."[xlix]

E. G. Larson, one of the deckhands who survived the wreck, said he was shocked when *PM 18* left port. The pumps were running constantly while she was moored in Ludington and kept on clanking as she pulled out into the lake. Why didn't the inspectors see it? Where was the water coming from?

There was speculation that maybe a broken deadlight (a.k.a. porthole) sunk the ship. There were deadlights

———————

very low on the hull, between the car deck and water line. R. G. Butler, a naval architect who helped construct *PM 18* said Kilty never would have left with a defective deadlight in this area. In any kind of storm, the waves regularly swept the area so having properly secured deadlights was very important. Butler instead believed she was over stressed on the summer runs damaging her hull. Captain Dionne from the Sheboygan Life-Saving Station thought she may have spun out her shaft and thus quickly flooded. He too blamed the summer cruising and lack of renovation in Ludington.[1]

However other men, including surviving crew, blamed an open deadlight. They claimed it was open for ventilation when she crossed from Chicago and left open when she departed for Milwaukee. It was claimed a Grand Trunk Railway car ferry was nearly lost when a low deadlight was left open. It took a super human effort by the crew to finally close and secure it. Everyone had a theory but none had an answer.

Survivors remembered the last minutes of the *PM 18*. Surviving porter Ray Bickford, related, "Just two or three minutes before the boat went down she began to settle rapidly and we knew she was sinking. Mrs. Turner was near me, fully clothed with a suit of Captain Kilty's clothes beneath one arm and her handbag under the other with a package containing some dresses. She had her prayer beads entwined about her fingers. I tried to tell her that she could not be loaded down like that in the water but she refused to cast them away and I took all away from her by force except the beads which she said she would not give up. The suit of the captain's clothes we had given her an half hour before that she might take off her dress and put them on as she would be better able to take care of herself with the man's clothes. We urged her several times to go to her cabin and change but she put it off too long."[li]

During the last minutes of *PM 18's* time on the surface many moments played out, some tragic, others comic and some greedy. An example of the latter involved Seymore Cochrane, the representative of the Chicago Navigation Company. He was returning to the city after officially turning *PM 18* over to the railroad after the summer's charter. In his charge was a bag containing $1,000, a fortune in 1910. Realizing he couldn't be burdened with it when the ship sank, he threw it on the boat deck and announced anyone could have it. Deckhand Joe Standing Bear grabbed the purse and tried to jam it under his lifejacket but it was too big. Instead he held it tight in his hand. When the boat lurched suddenly and dove for the bottom some of the men jumped for their lives. One of the survivors reported seeing Standing Bear flying through the air, still grasping the bag, evidently propelled by the force of air blowing out of the sinking ship. Neither Standing Bear or his new wealth survived.[lii]

PM General Superintendent in Ludington, Mr. Mercereau, said he had no idea why the ship filled with water but speculated the weight of sending the railcars off the stern could have added to the problems. Witnesses claimed when she dove for the bottom two cars were hung up on the stern, which certainly would have added to an out of trim position. He also denied Kilty was afraid to sail the ship. Again, PM spin control was vital.

Surprising for a newspaper, an editorial in the *Ludington Chronicle* suggested some very workmanlike points. The open stern type of ship must be eliminated. All deadlights below the car deck should be abolished. A wireless set that transmits but can't receive is unsatisfactory. The government should require any ship to have yearly hull inspection in a drydock. All were valid suggestions.[liii]

Once the funerals and memorial services finished recriminations started. Why did *PM 18* sink? Since every officer was lost with the ship, testimony could only be taken from the men and as in all such events, what they individually saw was just a small piece of the puzzle. An officer might have had a "bigger" picture.

Because she sank near the western shore of the lake, the U.S. government inspectors from Milwaukee took charge of the investigation. Inspectors Captain F. Van Patten and Captain W. Collins were in charge. The investigation was also closed to the public. Simon Burke, the wheelsman who survived the wreck, was one of the first to testify at the closed-door court of inquiry. Before going into the hearing, he said, "I don't know how it happened. The boat went down with a list to port and stern foremost and I was washed out through the starboard door, without having time to put on the life preserver that I had in my hand. It took only two minutes from the time the dynamos were flooded in the engine room for the water to reach the pilothouse. I went down twice, the suction taking me down to a great depth until the pressure of the water bruised me. I didn't hear or see anything. One of the boats from *No. 17* picked me up and brought me here. At 3:30 a.m. the engineer reported that we were taking water but the ship was acting all right. I changed the course four points to keep her before the wind. A half hour later the captain instructed me to head for shore, due west. The last time I saw him alive was at

5:00 a.m. when he said, "The boat's all right; we'll save her." He was dead when I saw him again." It was noted this was Burke's fifth shipwreck and he had every intention of sailing again.[liv]

The investigation was completed by September 19 and the confidential report forwarded to Captain C. H. Wescott, the Supervising Inspector in Detroit. However, Captain Collins stated to the papers that the cause of the accident, "has not been determined and he has doubts if this will ever be established in view of the fact that the wreck is inaccessible to divers."[lv]

The federal Supervising Inspector General in Washington, D. C., G. Uhler, stated the Grand Haven inspectors told him they couldn't determine the source of the leak either. Uhler concluded a sudden bursting of the steel bulkhead between the flicker and engine room was key to the quick sinking. The "flicker" is a term used for the crews quarters, located just below the car deck about midship. The term comes from the early days of the car ferries when electricity was a rare commodity. It seems some car-ferry sailors managed to rig a light in over the table where they played endless games of cards. Because the electric line was weak, the light "flickered" and thus was born the name.

Supervising Inspector, Captain C. H. Wescott, offered a different perspective on the wreck. "The officers and crew of the *Pere Marquette No. 18* which foundered in Lake Michigan were brave - too brave. They underestimated the seriousness of the situation and did not believe the boat would go down so soon. They made every precaution to quit the sinking car ferry but waited too long before doing so.

———————

"When that car ferry left its dock the day of the disaster it apparently was in the best of condition. The day before the local steamboat inspectors in Grand Haven had gone over it from top to bottom and had found nothing wrong. It was declared that the inspectors made that inspection in two hours. This is not the case, for I investigated this point very thoroughly.

"The inspectors went aboard about dinner time and did not wind up until about 9 o'clock. Had there been anything wrong at that time that inspection would have showed it."[lvi]

The Steamboat Inspection Service investigation couldn't determine what sank *PM 18* but it did suggest a couple of possibilities.

- It felt a broken deadlight was incapable of admitting enough water to account for the seven feet found aft by the oiler. The loss of other deadlights could still not admit enough water to cause her to founder.

- Perhaps a seacock was left open during the conversion from the excursion charter.

- Could the water have entered though an open 18-inch car deck scuttle?

- Nothing easily explained the sudden dive for the bottom unless a bulkhead gave way, but there was no direct evidence for this.[lvii]

Marine men didn't accept the open deck scuttle as a viable theory, pointing out the wind was northerly, striking the ferry on her starboard quarter making it unlikely she would ship seas aboard. They also felt even wide open scuttles would not admit enough water to sink her.[lviii]

Others laid the blame on her summer cruising. Perhaps she backed into a short piling, opening hull plates under her fantail. It was an area not easily seen so it is possible the injury escaped detection. Under calm lake conditions water never reached the damaged area but in the rough water of her first car ferry crossing loaded with heavy cars and sitting lower it the water, the damage was an opening to disaster.[lix]

Eventually the federal investigation provided someone to blame and it laid the fault for the loss of life at the feet of Captain Kilty. Since he was dead, there could be no rebuttal. "It is our opinion that . . . the master of the *Pere Marquette No. 18* showed very poor judgment in holding the crew aboard the boat as long as he did. As much as two hours before the vessel sank we think that his knowledge and ability as a seaman must have told him that his ferry was in a very precarious condition and most dangerous to be aboard of. We believe Capt. Kilty's efforts were directed more toward saving the ship than saving lives aboard his boat."[lx] The statement damns Kilty for not abandoning her sooner but does not imply why he had to leave her at all. So what was really the reason the *PM 18* sank?

Some good did come from the disaster. The operators of the Lake Michigan ferries met and decided to equip the vessels with sea gates to help protect the open sterns from boarding seas. Whether newly built or older ferries, all needed this protection. The first ferry retro fitted was *Ann Arbor No. 5*. Eventually all received sea gates. The companies also elected to use watertight hatches instead of open gratings on the car deck above the engineroom and coal bunkers.

With the loss of *PM 18* the company needed an immediate replacement and one was ordered from the American Ship Building Company. It was the only Lake Michigan car ferry ever built in Chicago and since the yard there was empty, construction started immediately. The new *PM 18 (II)* was built in 90 working days, a record for any of the Lake Michigan boats. In service by January 1911, her design was very close to the original *PM 18* with a few changes. The pilothouse was enclosed as opposed to being open and the passenger space was decreased.[lxi]

PM 18 (II) *was quickly built to replace* PM 18.
Stonehouse Collection

Footnotes
[i]Stonehouse Collection, *PM 18.*
[ii]*Ludington Chronicle*, September 14, 1910.
[iii]George W. Hilton, *Great Lakes Car Ferries*, (Berkeley, California: Howell- North, 1962), p. 166.
[iv]Hilton, *Great Lakes*, p. 125.

ᵛHilton, *Great Lakes*, pp. 126-127.
ᵛⁱHilton, *Great Lakes*, p. 127.
ᵛⁱⁱ*Ludington Chronicle*, March 27, 1907.
ᵛⁱⁱⁱ*Ludington Chronicle*, undated, 1907.
ⁱˣ*Ludington Chronicle*, undated, 1907.
ˣ*Ludington Chronicle*, June 26, 1907.
ˣⁱ*Ludington Chronicle*, July 10, 1907.
ˣⁱⁱ*Ludington Chronicle*, July 10, 1907.
ˣⁱⁱⁱ*Ludington Chronicle*, September 4, 1907.
ˣⁱᵛ*Chicago Record-Herald*, September 5, 1908.
ˣᵛ*Ludington Chronicle*, September 9, 1909.
ˣᵛⁱStonehouse Collection, *PM 18*.
ˣᵛⁱⁱ*Ludington Chronicle*, September 8, 1910.
ˣᵛⁱⁱⁱPete Caesar, *What Sunk the Pere Marquette 18,* (Great Lakes Shipwreck Research, 2005), p. 30.
ˣⁱˣ*Ludington Chronicle*, September 7, 1910.
ˣˣCaesar, *What Sunk*, p. 35.
ˣˣⁱStonehouse Collection, *PM 18*; the time is also given as 11:40 p.m.
ˣˣⁱⁱCaesar, *What Sunk*, p. 58; *Sunday Herald,* (Grand Rapids), September 11, 1910.
ˣˣⁱⁱⁱHilton, *Great Lakes*, pp. 131.
ˣˣⁱᵛ*Ludington Chronicle*, September 14, 1910.
ˣˣᵛSome sources claim up to 15 cars were dumped. Until the wreck is found and number aboard counted, the true number is unknown.
ˣˣᵛⁱStonehouse Collection; *Sunday Herald,* (Grand Rapids), September 11, 1910.
ˣˣᵛⁱⁱCaesar, *What Sunk*, p. 40. The flag at half-mast was unusual. The typical distress signal is the flag upside down; there is discussion *PM 17* never heard the CQD call but rather came across *PM 18* by accident.
ˣˣᵛⁱⁱⁱHilton, *Great Lakes*, 131.
ˣˣⁱˣCaesar, *What Sunk*, p. 60; *Sunday Herald,* (Grand Rapids), September 11, 1910.
ˣˣˣhttp://carferries.com/pmcarferries/*pm18*; *New York Times*, May 1, 1915.

[xxxi]*Sunday Herald,* (Grand Rapids), September 11, 1910.
[xxxii]*Ludington Record-Appeal*, September 15, 1910.
[xxxiii]*Ludington Record-Appeal*, September 15, 1910.
[xxxiv]*Ludington Chronicle*, September 14, 1910.
[xxxv]The accuracy of newspapers in 1910 was no better than today.
[xxxvi]Caesar, *What Sunk*, pp. 61-62.
[xxxvii]*Ludington Record-Appeal*, September 15, 1910.
[xxxviii]*Sunday Herald,* (Grand Rapids), September 11, 1910.
[xxxix]*Ludington Chronicle*, September 14, 1910.
[xl]*Ludington Chronicle*, September 14, 1910.
[xli]*Sunday Herald,* (Grand Rapids), September 11, 1910.
[xlii]*Ludington Chronicle*, September 14, 1910.
[xliii]*Ludington Chronicle*, October 5, 1910.
[xliv]*Grand Rapids Herald*, September 14, 1910.
[xlv]Stonehouse Collection, *PM 18*.
[xlvi]*Ludington Chronicle*, October 19, 1910.
[xlvii]Caesar, *What Sunk*, pp. 74-75.
[xlviii]*Kalamazoo Gazette*, September 14, 1910.
[xlix]*Muskegon News Chronicle*, September 13, 1910.
[l]Caesar, *What Sunk*, pp. 79-80.
[li]*Sunday Herald,* (Grand Rapids), September 11, 1910; *Ludington Chronicle*, September 14, 1910. There is some dispute regarding the tale. One source says the deckhand was lost and another that he survived but lost the bag of money.
[lii]*Sunday Herald,* (Grand Rapids), September 11, 1910.
[liii]*Ludington Chronicle*, September 14, 1910.
[liv]*Milwaukee Journal*, September 10, 1910.
[lv]*Milwaukee Journal*, September 19, 1910.
[lvi]*Ludington Chronicle*, September 21, 1910.
[lvii]Stonehouse Collection, *PM 18*.
[lviii]*Ludington Chronicle*, September 14, 1910.
[lix]*Ludington Chronicle*, September 14, 1910.
[lx]*Ludington Chronicle*, October 5, 1910.
[lxi]Stonehouse Collection, *PM 18*.

✳ 2

ARLINGTON

Did he or didn't he?
May 1, 1940

Do captain's really go down with their ships or is it just a popular legend? In the case of the Canadian steamer *Arlington*, Captain Frederick J. Burke did take the final plunge with his ship but the question is whether he really wanted to or simply was too late getting off?

The vessel was built in 1913 as the *F. P. Jones* at Wyandotte, Michigan for the George Hall Coal Company. At 244-feet long, with a beam of 43-feet, she was designed to navigate the narrow confines of the old Welland Canal. Her top speed light (without cargo) was 12 mph and loaded, 10.2 mph. During 1918-19 she sailed salt water operating for the U. S. Shipping Board, coming back to the Hall Company in 1919. In 1920 she was sold to James Playfair, transferred Canadian and renamed the *Glencadam*. For a time, she operated in the Caribbean as a sugar hauler but was not successful in the trade and returned to the Lakes. The Mathews Steamship Company purchased her in 1925, renaming her *Arlington*. When the Depression bankrupted Mathews she was sold to the Colonial Steamships Ltd. and in 1936 the Burke Towing and Salvage Company of Midland, Ontario purchased her.[i]

The Arlington was launched as the F. P. Jones in 1913. Stonehouse Collection

When she left Port Arthur on Lake Superior at 12:08 p.m. on April 30, 1940, World War II was a bare six months old but grain prices were climbing, making it well worthwhile for even a small vessel like the *Arlington* to take the trade. Her holds were filled with nearly 98,000 bushels of northern Manitoba hard wheat bound for Owen Sound on Georgian Bay. Later testimony showed the cargo was properly stowed and in fact virtually filled the holds to the top of the hatches. Because of the volume, shifting boards were not used. To keep her steady with the relatively light wheat, she carried water ballast in her tanks as was typically done.[ii]

There was no suggestion the small steamer was not seaworthy in all respects. On April 16 she was inspected by Henry William Morris, surveyor for the American Bureau of Shipping who found her in good order with no deficiencies. Her hatch covers were all in good condition and she had adequate equipment to secure them, including

In 1920 the Jones *was sold to Playfield and renamed* Glencadam. *Stonehouse Collection*

windbars and double tarps. Four days later William MacKenzie, a steamship inspector who had checked the vessel annually since 1922, assessed her hull, machinery and boilers. He found her also in good condition.[iii]

On June 16, 1939 she was drydocked for repair and inspection. August saw her back in the yard after grounding near Collins Inlet, Ontario. Such accidents were not uncommon to a hardworking vessel.

When the *Arlington* left Port Arthur on the 30th, it was her second trip of the season.[iv] The first was made without incident. The wheat arrived dry, evidence the hatches were well sealed.

It was a little unusual a small ship like the *Arlington* took a direct route to the Soo considering the less than ideal weather forecast. She could have run the north shore and been protected from the predicted north-northeast winds. Smaller ships and larger ones too, often followed the north route in the spring and fall.

The *Arlington* passed Passage Island at the northern tip of Isle Royale at approximately 5:28 p.m. A fresh north-northeast breeze was blowing accompanied by a little light snow. Some ice formed on the ship but nothing to speak of. The sea was moderate. The weather report received prior to departing Port Arthur gave no indication of anything to worry about. All it all, the conditions were typical for early spring on Superior.

Around 11:30 p.m. the wireless operator on the *Arlington* received an updated forecast. "Lake Superior– fresh north-east to north winds; mostly cloudy and cold with light snow falls and flurries; Thursday, fair and cool." The operator noted the message and left it on his work desk. He didn't bother to give it to Captain Burke.

The Arlington *shortly before her loss.*
Stonehouse Collection

The captain always ignored weather forecasts received enroute. Why would it be any different now?

Still it wasn't a bad forecast so the steamer would just continue on her way whether he gave it to Burke or not.^v

The forecast however was sadly optimistic. When the mate came on duty at 12:15 a.m. May 1, 1940, the wind was already blowing at gale force! None-the-less, it didn't become dangerous until about 3:30 a.m. when he noticed the tarp on number 5 hatch was loose. A loose tarp meant the hatch was no longer watertight and boarding seas could begin to flood into the cargo hold. The mate called Burke to the pilothouse.

This was Burke's second trip to the pilothouse during the mate's watch. Shortly after he came on duty the mate turned the ship before the wind to better examine the hatch covers but Burke, sensing the change in heading, came up and ordered her back on the original course. He remained in the pilothouse for an hour or so before returning to his cabin. Clearly he didn't trust the mate's decision making ability. As the gale increased, the speed of the *Arlington* decreased to 7 mph. It was the best she could do punching into the building seas.

When Burke came back up at 3:30 a.m. he took over while the mate led a group of men on deck to try to secure the hatches. This was very dangerous work. The *Arlington* did not have a lifeline rigged fore and aft on the spar deck so there was nothing for the men to tie off safety lines to. A lifeline was aboard and the proper hooks installed, but Burke never ordered it rigged. Apparently he didn't believe in such gear. The ship's course also put her in the trough of the seas and coupled with her low 3-1/2 foot of freeboard, meant waves regularly swept over the deck. The mate later claimed at times the waves were 10 to 20 feet high. The second mate nearly went overboard when a wave smashed into him.

When the mate's work party reached the number 3 hatch the tarp was turned back two feet and the tarp on number 5 was half off and windbars bent. Wedges holding the tarps tight were also gone, washed away by the battering waves. The first mate determined it was impossible to make repairs given the terrible conditions on deck. He did not return to the pilothouse or tell Burke. The captain wouldn't care anyway. He was known as a heavy weather sailor who trusted his ship to just gut it out regardless of the weather.

The ship was not sounded for water entering after 11:30 p.m. To take a sounding it was necessary to go on deck and after 12:15 a.m. it was too dangerous to do so. In other words Burke had no idea if his ship was taking water, or if she was, how much?

The first sure knowledge water was entering the ship was when the fireman in the engine room saw it coming in from the upper corner of the "watertight" bulkhead port side between the compartment and cargo hold. He could plainly hear a creaking like rivets popping loose of the bulkhead as it was expanding under the water pressure. The Canadian investigators concluded the sea pounding on the bulkhead eventually caused it to give way allowing a torrent of water that soon put out the boiler fire. Since there was no telephone between the engine room and pilothouse and going on the open weather deck was suicidal, Burke never knew what was happening in this most critical part of the ship. Regardless of the danger the engineers stood to their posts until the end. When the fires went out, they fled topside.

By 3:30 a.m. the *Arlington* had a slight list, estimated by the engineer at about 5 degrees. It slowly grew until forty-five minutes later Burke signaled for half speed. It was an empty gesture. When the list reached 30 degrees the lifeboat was launched. Burke ordered no action to counter the list, for example flooding the tanks on the opposite side of the ship. While the steamer carried two lifeboats aft, due to the heavy starboard list, the port boat could not be lowered and was left secure in the davits.[vi]

The situation on the *Arlington* slowly deteriorated without any action being taken by Burke. He never issued orders or took command of the situation. It is almost like he was in shock, unable to give the orders a captain must to save either ship or sailors.

———————

That Burke was the only casualty was largely the
result of the mate taking charge forward and the engineer
aft. When it became apparent the ship was sinking, the
mate alerted the men forward to get ready to abandon
ship. No instructions came from Burke for anything.
When the wheelsman realized the ship was no longer
responding to the helm, he left the pilothouse and did not
return. He told the master he was going below and asked
if he was coming. When he received no reply he ran
down the open spar deck to the lifeboat. Burke surely
must have been aware of the situation since when the
engine room flooded out, the second engineer rang the
pilothouse on the telegraph signaling the engines were
dead, but without a telephone he couldn't explain the
situation. The engineer gathered his men aft and led
them to the lifeboat.[vii]

Boat drills were only partially conducted on the
Arlington. The boats were swung out on the davits but
not lowered into the water. Although this was common
practice for many commercial vessels, it did little to
prepare the crews for an emergency.

Canadian investigators later concluded the ship
foundered because of water flooding partially through the
number 3 and 5 hatches and the failure of the bulkhead
between the freeboard deck and poop deck. The bulkhead
divided the engineroom and cargo hold number 2.

The *Arlington* sank about 110 miles on a direct line
from Port Arthur and 10 miles southeast of Superior Shoal.
Luckily for the crew the Canadian Steamship Line vessel
Collingwood was just behind them and Captain T. J.
Carson was keeping an eye on her. The 386-foot
Collingwood followed behind since Port Arthur. He could

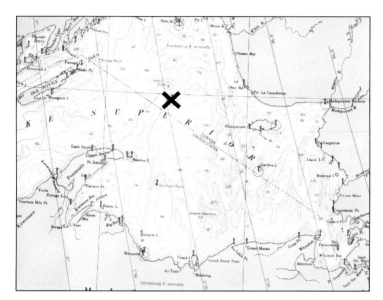

plainly see she was having trouble in the gale but it wasn't until she suddenly dove for the bottom, 800-feet below, he knew how serious the situation was. He skillfully brought his larger vessel up to the lifeboat and sheltering it in his lee, was able to bring all 16 survivors aboard. The lifeboat had been in the water a bare 15 minutes.

The *Collingwood* continued on for Midland on Lake Huron where she landed the survivors. As the *Collingwood* didn't have a wireless, the first public knowledge of the disaster was when she reached the Soo. Alerted by the newspapers, 600-700 people watched as the steamer pulled into her dock and the survivors came ashore. The crew was quickly bundled to the town hall to testify in front of Captain F. S. Slocombe of Toronto, Supervising Examiner of Masters and Mates in the Inland Division of the Dominion Department of Transport. Two of the survivors, Francis (Fat) Swales, 17 and his friend

The big Canada Steamship Lines freighter Collingwood
rescued the Arlington *crew. Stonehouse Collection*

Ted Brodeur, both Midland junior hockey teammates,
said it was only because Burke was a hockey fan they
were hired as deckhands. The pair also said it was their
first and last trip. "I never expected to see such weather
as we encountered Tuesday night," said Brodeur. He also
related, "The *Collingwood's* men looked after us swell,
but I don't think I'll ever go on a boat again" W. S. Lee,
the *Arlington* wireless operator, remarked that Captain
Burke told him not to send an SOS because the
Collingwood was close by.

Captain Carson spoke briefly with Burke's brothers
when he docked at Midland and related what he knew of
the *Arlington's* last minutes. Carson was badly affected
by the tragedy. When he went to the dock elevators to
brief his employers he was weeping and holding his head.
Later he went to his home and into seclusion.

The Canadian investigators, considering that Burke
was dead, were exceptionally kind to him in their report.
They made various excuses for his action, suggesting he

made an error in judgment in continuing his course after the gale developed, but yet claiming he should not be blamed for the mistake. They also thought Burke may not have known the true situation, after all the mate never told him of the unsecured hatches and the engineer could not communicate the engine room was flooding. The steamer had also blown around to southwest, heading nearly opposite her intended track. In this writer's evaluation, such a whitewash is unbelievable! A captain of Burke's reputation and experience couldn't have been so "clueless" concerning his ship. Considering the list, loss of power, sluggishness and failure to respond to the helm, he had to know what was happening. As the ship settled deeper into the lake, several hatch covers blew off, and a sea of grain erupted into the air. Clearly the ship was heading for the bottom, NOW! But Burke did nothing!

After the lifeboat was already launched, Burke came out of the pilothouse, slipped coming down the steps and partially fell, picked himself up and held up a hand to the men in the lifeboat. He opened the door to his cabin and went in. The investigating commissioner believed he was signaling the lifeboat to wait while he went to get a lifejacket, ship's papers or personal effects. Once he entered the cabin the ship's list increased and the investigator thought he could have been tumbled into a corner of the cabin and unable to escape. He was known to be a very "large" man. Perhaps his bulk hindered his movement. The *Arlington* sank within two minutes of Burke entering his cabin.[viii] The lifeboat was only 50-feet away from the steamer when she sank. Had Burke jumped, it is likely he would have been quickly picked up.[ix] Again, Burke did nothing.

As the result of the circumstance of his death, the captain going down with his ship, all sorts of tales have developed around his actions. One claims he waved a final good bye to his crew then retreated to his cabin to meet death alone. Another says he stayed behind to control the ship to allow the lifeboat to launch and escape with his crew. Since the ship was already drifting without power, this is obviously fantasy.

Captain Burke's brothers David and Edward, both Great Lakes captains, offered a $500 reward for the recovery of his body. It was apparently never claimed.[x] Burke joined his ship on the bottom of the lake.

Around the Lakes Burke was often called "Tatey Bug." It seems as a child his family called him "Teddy" but Burke was unable to pronounce it clearly. It always came out "Tatey," thus his nickname. Where Bug came from is unknown, but perhaps was a play on his large size. He was well known as a heavy weather sailor, willing to tough it out when other captains took shelter. He started sailing with logging tugs and as he gained experience moved up to big steamers like the *Genlivet*, *Glenorchy*, *Gleniffer*, *James Eads* and *Ralph Budd*. Burke Towing and Wrecking consisted only of a couple of tugs and barges, plus the *Arlington*. It was in effect a one vessel fleet and she was intended to be the big profit producer.[xi] Ship and cargo were a loss of $130,000.[xvi]

Burke enjoyed an excellent reputation for keeping a cool head in an emergency. It was a reputation at odds with his performance on the *Arlington*. On October 29, 1924, he was captain of the steamer *Glenorchy* downbound from Fort William with wheat heading for the Welland Canal and Montreal. About noon the ship was in pea soup fog six miles off Harbor Beach on Lake Huron. The *Glenorchy* was running at half speed when the faint sound of fog signal reached Burke on the wing of the pilothouse. It was unclear which direction the blasts were coming from. At 1:30 p.m. the steamer struck the upbound steamer *Leonard B. Miller* bow to bow. The *Glenorchy* was fatally wounded and sinking fast. The *Miller* came alongside and crew leaped to safety. After counting off his crew Burke discovered two were missing. Jumping back aboard the rapidly sinking steamer he discovered one trapped in a cabin and the other laying injured. Freeing the trapped man, Burke took both to the *Miller* moments before the *Glenorchy* dove for the bottom.[xii] By any standard, he was hero.

The *Glenorchy* rests in approximately 120-feet of water and has been explored by scuba divers.[xiii]

Given his long experience as a master and reputation as a heavy weather sailor, what happened to turn him into an indecisive recluse, failing to provide any leadership to his men, refusing to work to secure loose hatches or even save his own life? This is the real mystery of the wreck. What turned a brave, resourceful captain into a weak and limp jellyfish?

The *Arlington* was Burke's third shipwreck. As a young man he experienced a tugboat burning and sinking and of course there was the big *Glenorchy* in Lake Huron. It was claimed the chief engineer had gone through four sinkings. Perhaps the combination of the two men equaled a shipboard "Jonah?"[xv]

———————

Footnotes

[i]Rev. Peter Van der Linden, *Great Lakes Ships We Remember, Volume One*, (Cleveland: Freshwater Press, 1979), p. 35.

[ii]Report to the Honourable Minister of Transport re. Investigation into the foundering of the *S.S. Arlington*, May 30, 1940.

[iii]Report to the Honourable.

[iv]Port Arthur and Fort William are now Thunder Bay.

[v]Report to the Honourable.

[vi]Report to the Honourable.

[vii]Report to the Honourable.

[viii]Report to the Honourable.

[ix]*Arlington* file, Stonehouse Collection.

[x]*Great Lakes Journal*, June 3, 1940.

[xi]Dwight Boyer, *True Tales of the Great Lakes*, (New York: Dodd, Mead and Company, 1971), pp. 1-16.

[xii]*Globe and Mail*, (Toronto), October 31, 1924; *Daily Star*, (Toronto), October 31, 1924.

[xiii]http://www.goodiving.com/locationdetails.asp?id=2256.

[xiv]*Shipping Casualties, Return for Wrecks*, 1940, Ship *Arlington*.

[xv]Boyer, *True Tales*, p. 19.

✳ 3

JOHN M. MCKERCHEY

She's flooding forward!

Many kinds of vessels earned a living on the Great Lakes. Some were graceful schooners, with towering masts piled high with billowing clouds of canvas. Others were mighty steel freighters plowing their way through the waves carrying heavy cargos of rich iron ore. Ornate sidewheel steamers with rolling black smoke pouring from tall stacks and lowly fish tugs all earned their keep at various times of history. There were also unusual craft like sand suckers, spending careers harvesting sand from the bottom of the lakes and rivers for industrial use. The *S.S. John M. McKerchey* was such a vessel. In fact it is claimed she was the first vessel equipped not only for dredging sand and gravel, but also to carry coal and stone.

The 506 gross ton *McKerchey*, owned by the Kelleys Island Lime and Transport Company, was built in 1906. At 161.2 feet in length and 37.1 feet in beam, she was a small vessel but well suited to her trade. And as a function of her design she had the ability to self-load and self-unload either sand or gravel. Her twin engines could propel her at a slow but economical 8 miles per hour fully loaded.

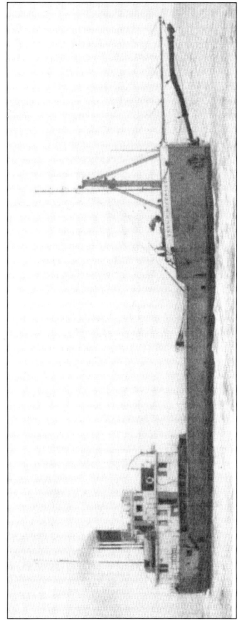

The McKerchey was owned by the Kelleys Island Lime and Transport company.
Stonehouse Collection

The loading was accomplished through a 15-inch diameter hose mounted on the forward part of the vessel and operated by a diesel suction pump. The hose came through the hull on the port bow. A cable falls arrangement lowered it to the lake bottom and hauled it back aboard. When finished the hose was disconnected from the suction pipe and the hole through the hull made watertight with a couple of large plates. Making everything seaworthy was a fair amount of work, but necessary considering the vessel's low freeboard and method of operation. The sand and gravel sucked from the lake bottom was dumped into an open cargo hold which typically contained about 750 cubic yards of material. Fully loaded, the material came flush with the top of the hold. Unloading was accomplished with a 60-foot boom and clamshell bucket. When not in use the boom was stored on a cradle over the center of the cargo hold. There were also three tanks, or water bottoms, running lengthwise below the cargo hold. The sand and gravel she pulled from the lake was used in a variety of manufacturing and construction projects.

On October 15, 1950, the *McKerchey* was at the pumping ground located about seven and three-quarters mile, 279 degrees true from west breakwater at Lorain, Ohio. At 1:15 a.m. on the 16th she left the grounds, heading for Lorain. The weather was clear with a moderate wind and sea running from the southeast. Waves were striking the vessel on the port bow in the area where the suction pipe went through the hull plating. Wind and waves were well within safe operating limits.

Roughly half an hour later, the watchman discovered water pouring into the forepeak, already reaching a depth

The McKerchey *with her boom and pipe secured.*
Stonehouse Collection

of three to four feet. He hurriedly told the captain who instructed him to find the chief engineer and get the ballast pump going. Soon the pump was thumping hard, sending a geyser of water back into the lake. Meanwhile the second mate ran below to the forepeak compartment to check on the progress. Instead of closing and securing the hatch, he left it open and reported the situation to the captain, then roused the crew from their bunks ordering them to clear and lower the lifeboat and raft. A fast sounding of the tanks showed 13-feet of water in the number three starboard tank and increasing fast. All the while the *McKerchey* slowly listed to starboard.

The first assistant engineer, who was also on duty, ran forward to see what was happening. He was horrified to see the forepeak had filled and water was running knee deep onto the deck. It was pouring out of the casing around the suction pipe, running over the raised deck and into the number one starboard tank. Strangely the watertight doors leading to the forepeak were all open and water was flooding deep into the bowels of the vessel.

The engineer called the pilothouse and was told by the captain, Horace Johnson, he thought he could beach her and was heading for shore. About this time, someone, likely the captain, threw the alarm switch and bells began to ring. He also called the Coast Guard lifeboat station at Lorain, asking them to come out and standby. Minutes later a 36-foot motor lifeboat, CG-36348 was underway followed quickly by another 36-footer, CG-36357.[1] The *McKerchey* continued to increase her starboard list. Meanwhile most of the crew took to the lifeboat or raft not willing to take a chance if she went over. Sensing the danger of her imminent roll, the assistant engineer crawled out the port side engine room door and waited for the end on the open deck. When she finally capsized, he jumped into the lake and was eventually rescued by the Coast Guard. The engines were still running when the sand sucker went "bottom up".

The *McKerchey* capsized at 02:30 a.m., a mile from the Lorain breakwater and just a few minutes before the

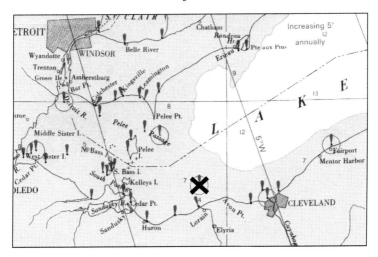

first Coast Guard motor lifeboat arrived. Quickly the first five crewmen were hauled out of the lake. The rest were safe in either the vessel's lifeboat or raft. They were soon transferred to one of the Coast Guard boats and taken to shore. Five of the men went to a local hospital to be checked over although none were seriously injured.

When a head count was taken the only man missing from the 20-man crew was the captain. Apparently he went down with his ship. In the odd chance the Coast Guard missed him in the dark one of the boats continued to patrol the area and also warned other shipping clear of the wreck. Approximately four feet of her port bilge remained above water, a real hazard to any vessel in the area. Late that afternoon the Merritt, Chapman, Scott and Company tug *William A. Whitney* arrived and her diver recovered the body of the captain from the wreck. Eventually the wreck settled until the highest point was six feet below the surface.

The Coast Guard board of investigation chewed over the disaster and reached a number of conclusions including:

1. The question of why the master died was undetermined. There was plenty of time to get off safely. Did he decide to stay to the end in a desperate attempt to save his vessel by beaching her regardless of the quickly developing list? Did he gamble with his own life or did he just fail to appreciate how quickly the situation was spinning out of control?

2. How the water initially entered the forepeak could not be determined but once her head was

below the suction hose opening the situation was hopeless.

3. It was the second mate's responsibility to assure, "all scuttles, doors, and so forth were closed. He saw water coming through the forepeak scuttle hatch but made no effort to close and clamp down the door... had the second mate closed down the scuttle hatch leading down to the forepeak and the watertight door on the casing, there was a chance of the vessel making Lorain Harbor or a possibility of beaching the vessel. Therefore a charge of Inattention to Duty is being preferred against... the second mate."

4. Vessels in the sand trade should be dry docked for inspection at least every two years and the appropriate regulations should be so changed. However the Commandant of the Coast Guard, who had the responsibility of reviewing all board recommendations, disagreed, claiming the marine inspectors had the authority to require a vessel to be dry docked for inspection whenever they feel it necessary, thus a formal change to regulation was not needed.[ii]

The *McKerchey* wasn't the only sand sucker lost in Lake Erie. The *Hansen*, *Kelley Island* and *Sand Merchant* also eventually found their way to the bottom. None were especially seaworthy and when placed in a difficult situation through storm or accident, usually sank.

The *John M. McKerchey* was named for Mr. John M. McKerchey a Detroit businessman and ship owner. A self made man, he started as a newsboy and telegraph

The McKerchey *unloading at a dock. The suction pipe is clearly visible along the rail.* Stonehouse Collection

messenger, learned the plumbing and steam fitting trade engaging in it for sixteen years; later sold builders and pavers' supplies and eventually became a ship owner.

The *McKerchey* wreck was considered a hazard to navigation and dynamited to clear the harbor entrance. And so ended the career of a small but colorful member of the Great Lakes fleet.

Sand sucking operations were also popular in the Detroit area including the St. Clair River and Lake St. Clair. These were the original "dredging grounds" for the *McKerchey*. Many old vessels were fitted out with cranes and pumps and sent out to recover sand from the large beds in the St. Clair River. It was very lucrative until the shoreline owners discovered "riparian rights" which gave them bottomland ownership to the middle of the rivers. Soon the sand companies were paying property owners 8-10 cents a yard, pretty good money in 1915 or so. Many operators found it cheaper to harvest (take) the "free" sand from the lake.

Footnotes

[i]Coast Guard small boat numbers translate as "36", a 36-foot in length and "357" being the serial number. The same methodology applies to all Coast Guard small boats.

[ii]Marine Board of Investigation; *SS John M. McKerchey*, foundering with loss of life, vicinity of Lorain Harbor, Ohio on 16 October 1950; http://www.usgennet.org/usa/mi/county/tuscola/det/detmck-mcm.htm; http://www.webandwire.com/coast%20guard%20casualties.htm; Rev. Peter Van der Linden, *Great Lakes Ships We Remember*, (Cleveland: Freshwater Press, 1979), p. 254.

HENRY STEINBRENNER

"When I saw the hatch covers blowing across the deck, I knew it was all over."[i]
May 11, 1953

When the 427-foot *Henry Steinbrenner* loaded with 6,800 tons of iron ore pulled away from the Great Northern Railway dock at Superior, Wisconsin there was no reason to suspect her trip down to Lake Erie and the Bethlehem Steel mills would be anything but routine. It was shortly after 5:00 a.m. (E.S.T.) on May 10, 1953 and over eight years since the last American freighter sank on the Lakes.[ii] The feeling of complacency was reinforced by the weather. It was magnificent with sunny skies and temperatures in the mid-70s; especially good for the upper Lakes so early in the year.

The *Steinbrenner* was owned by the Kinsman Transportation Company. At 52 years of age she was the oldest vessel in the fleet and among the smallest carriers on the Lakes. By no means however was she unduly old for lake service. Many vessels sailing were far older.

Lake Superior was nearly flat with hardly a ripple to break the surface. Later Captain Albert Stiglin, master of the *Steinbrenner*, recalled it was "smoother than a

The 427-foot Henry Steinbrenner *was 52 years old when lost. Stonehouse Collection*

pond."[iii] The forecast at 6:00 a.m. indicated a change, calling for southeast to south winds at 30 - 35 mph with occasional thunder squalls in Superior's west half. The lake would get decidedly choppy, but nothing the *Steinbrenner* couldn't handle with ease. The captain and his 30-man crew confidently began the run.

Stiglin, from Vermilion, Ohio, commanded the *Steinbrenner* for the first time this season, but he sailed with the Kinsman line for 16 of his 27-year career.[iv] 46 years old, he held master's papers for seven years.[v] For the previous four he captained the steamer *Phillip Minch*.[vi]

The *Steinbrenner* was routinely secured for sea. Her dozen cargo hatches were closed and fastened with Mulholland type clamps. There were 28 clamps on each hatch, although some of the steel screw threads were reportedly stripped. Ominously her heavy tarpaulins were not fitted over the hatches. Fitting tarps was a difficult and time consuming process, usually omitted unless conditions were expected to be very bad. It was a decision to be later regretted. The chock and hawse pipe covers were also fitted into place. All steering and navigation equipment with the exception of her radar were in operating order.[vii]

Albert Stiglin captained the Steinbrenner *on her last trip.*
Stonehouse Collection

The *Steinbrenner's* trip was uneventful until about 3:00 p.m. on May 10 when the wind freshened and the sea began to build. About 4:30 p.m. the first wave came aboard the ship, washing over the weather deck. With the weather deteriorating the crew hooked up to the lifeline and braved the open deck to recheck the hatches, chock and hawse pipe covers. Weather forecasts were still calling for south to southeast winds although now with a slight increase to 30 to 40 mph.

By 5:00 p.m. the weather had turned bad enough that only a quarter of the crew could make it to the galley for supper. The best the cooks could do was rustle up a cold meal anyway. Working in a ship's galley with a storm raging was both difficult and dangerous. [viii]

At 8:00 p.m. the pilothouse watch observed a hatch leaf on the port side of the number 11 hatch had worked loose. With the decks occasionally swept by seas, the cargo hold was open for flooding, a very perilous situation.

Third mate George Wiseman and three deck hands rigged traveling lines from the main deck lifeline cable and worked their way out to the wild open deck to secure the loose hatch leaf. Again and again the men were inundated by the cold gray waves rolling and crashing up the entire length of the deck. Without the lifelines they would have been lost overboard. During the struggle with the heavy steel hatch leaf, one of the men was swept through the open hatch falling 15 feet into the cargo hold. The others were able to haul him back on deck with his safety line. He was quickly bundled off to the galley - mess deck to recover. Luckily he was only bruised and battered, with no broken bones. The men then returned to the deck and finished securing the hatch. However the clamps were left only hand tightened.

The growing waves smashing down the deck prevented the mate and his men from returning forward, forcing them to shelter in the aft deckhouse. Unlike modern freighters, the *Steinbrenner* had no passageways fore and aft through the cargo holds. The only route was over the weather deck and with the raging gale it was a sure way to a watery death.

By 11:00 p.m. the *Steinbrenner* was beleaguered by a full lake storm. The east-northeast wind was gusting to 80 mph and seas continuing to build. Later a wild-eyed survivor claimed the seas grew to over 60-feet. More accurate estimates placed them at 20 feet plus, although some news accounts stated 30-35 feet.[ix]

Some of the crew didn't think the Steinbrenner *was seaworthy.* Stonehouse Collection

The Steinbrenner *taking water over the decks.*
Stonehouse Collection

The midnight weather forecast was finally beginning to catch up with the actual conditions. It predicted winds shifting to the northeast and blowing 45-50 mph, with intermittent thunder squalls.

Conditions in the open lake however were far worse. The steamer was pounded continuously and the waves were climbing on board and constantly covering her hatches. With the *Steinbrenner* heading into the wind, the seas were sweeping aboard from both sides, swirling over and down the weather deck, around the aft deckhouse to the fantail. To ride easier, the steamer checked down her speed to about 4.8 mph. Al Augsburger, an oiler deep in the engine room remembered water coming down her stack during the height of the storm![x]

Sometime around 4:30 a.m. the hatch leaf on the number 11 hatch again worked loose but now sea conditions were so severe it was impossible for anyone to go on deck. Instead both ballast pumps were started and suction taken on both port and starboard sides of the number 4 cargo hold. Stiglin later observed "...Cold water was pouring in over both sides of the ship. There was no way to stay on deck." [xi]

One of the deck hands who earlier assisted securing the hatches remembered, "water was pouring into the number 11 hatch at the stern. Every time she rolled, the hatch would roll and water poured in."[xii]

By 6:00 a.m. May 11, the pilothouse crew noticed the *Steinbrenner* was becoming sluggish and not responding well to her rudder. An hour later they saw other hatch covers working loose. If the ship was to be saved, fast action was needed to secure them. Clearly the pumps were unable to handle the flooding and the vessel was slowly settling deeper and deeper into the water. Accordingly the captain gave her full power to try to bring her around to the opposite course and provide the aft end of the weather deck enough shelter to allow crewmen to secure the hatches. Hopefully this would also slow the flooding, allowing the pumps to catch up. The maneuver did no good. The seas continued to wash over her deck with grasping malevolence. Venturing on deck meant a quick trip to Davy Jones' locker. After ten minutes the *Steinbrenner* came back around on the original course but only after spending several terrifying minutes rolling in the deadly trough of the waves.[xiii]

About 6:30 a.m. May 11, a sea crashed through one of the forecastle deck observation room doors. Quickly two men secured the door back in place by jamming heavy planking behind it. An hour later (a wave broke the door open again and again) it was secured. A third sea ripped out the two-inch thick door, hinges, jam, bracing and lock intact! The seas also found entry through the port chock in the windless room. Later one of the crew claimed the battering of the waves was so powerful, the pilothouse shifted three feet forward![xiv] Others claimed the four by 12 inch door bracing timber was "snapped like match sticks" and the waves, "were 60 feet high."[xv]

Shortly past 7:00 a.m., after she was back on her original heading, the captain broadcast a call for help on the radio and alerted the crew to put on their lifejackets. Six vessels, including the 650-foot *Wilfred Sykes*, the Hanna fleet 714-foot *Joseph H. Thompson*, 580-foot *D.M. Clemson*, *D.G. Kerr*, *William E. Cory*, *Ontadoc*, and *Hochelaga* all heard the call and headed for the scene. The *Thompson*, a converted WWII troopship, was the largest vessel on the Lakes at the time.[xvi] The *Clemson*, *Kerr* and *Cory* were all Pittsburgh Steamship

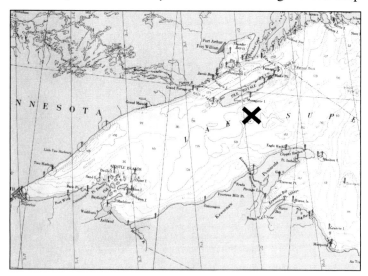

The D.G. Kerr *participated in the* Steinbrenner *rescue.*
Stonehouse Collection

Company vessels and were in the general vicinity of the Apostle Islands when the distress call was heard. Immediately all three turned north, throttled up to full power and headed for the sinking *Steinbrenner*. Wisely they also spread out to have a better chance of finding drifting survivors. Considering the very cold water, estimated at 35 degrees by some, time was critical.[xvii]

The Joseph H. Thompson *was the biggest freighter on the lakes in 1953.* Stonehouse Collection

Half an hour later three aft hatch covers (10, 11, 12) came loose. The general alarm was immediately sounded and the captain rang up "stop" on the Chadburn. The engine room answered as procedure called for and the *Steinbrenner* started to loose way or forward motion. Another MAYDAY call was made, now giving the position as 15 miles due south of Isle Royale Light. By now the engine room flooded out and water reached the grate threatening the red-hot boiler.[xviii] Mate David Kinnear of Inland Steel's *Sykes* remembered the distress call as, "We're awash. I think I am going to founder."[xix]

Six minutes later, at 7:36 a.m., the captain sounded the abandon ship signal of seven short blasts of the whistle and one long. The steamer was going down quickly and Stiglin wanted his men off her now! At the forward end ten of the crew gathered around the life raft on the forecastle deck. Aft the men stood by on the boat deck and on signal attempted to launch the 20 man lifeboats. The starboard or Number One boat launched with seven men aboard but the men remaining were not able to launch the port boat, apparently it jammed in it's davits.

As a last resort the port boat was unshackled from the falls. When the *Steinbrenner* suddenly sank stern first the boat floated clear although one of the two men working inside trying to insert the bottom plug was thrown out. The remaining man was slammed across the boat by the violent action and fatally injured. Later two crewmen managed to swim to the safety of the waterlogged and damaged boat.

Meanwhile forward, standing at the life raft, Captain Stiglin clearly remembered the events. ". . . I saw the two lifeboats clear the ship. I know that all men were clear for

I caught a brief glimpse of the two boats clear of the aft deck. The nine men and I climbed on the forecastle life raft as the ship sank lower and lower. When the raft started to float a wave capsized it and we lost four men for only six climbed back on the raft.ˣˣ

Considered by the Coast Guard as capable of carrying 15 persons, the six-foot by 12-foot life raft was made of medal air tanks with a wood frame top. Although it kept the men relatively above the water, it offered virtually no protection. They were constantly drenched by the freezing water and chilled by the racing wind.

When the raft capsized, Captain Stiglin landed in the water and was partially sucked under by the sinking steamer. He finally surfaced directly under the raft. After a struggle, he managed to climb back aboard.

One of the survivors, 19-year old Kenneth Kumm of Tonawanda, New York, later remembered, "I was ready to dive in and swim ashore when I saw Isle Royale. I was standing on the rail ready to jump when one of the boys grabbed me and said the waters too cold, you'll never make it. Then I got hit by a big wave and that's what saved me. It washed me right down to the middle of the ship. I remember opening my eyes underwater. . . I guess I passed over four or five hatches. When I came up for air and started swimming I was only ten feet from the lifeboat. The ship sank right as I reached the lifeboat."ˣˣⁱ

The *Steinbrenner* didn't break on the surface, apparently diving for the bottom 600 plus feet down in one piece. She must have hit with terrific impact. Since the wreck has never been found, her condition is unknown.

The men in the lifeboat claimed as the aft deck disappeared beneath the waves, the still red-hot boilers

---

exploded from contact with the ice water and debris flew threw the air.[xxii] Kenneth Kumm was swimming when the boiler went off and he actually felt a flash of heat pass through the icy water.[xxiii]

As the number one lifeboat was drifting past the stern of the *Steinbrenner*, one of the men looked up and saw an assistant engineer standing at the stern of the ship just looking down at them, making no effort to leave the sinking ship. The observer in the lifeboat thought this was most peculiar.[xxiv] Evidently some of the crew preferred to take their chances sticking with the ship rather than leaving her. The feeling was indeed prevalent of, "what the hell good is that little lifeboat when the big one goes down."[xxv]

The survivors in the number 1 lifeboat spent a cold, wet and miserable four and a half hours before being rescued at approximately 11:00 a.m. Originally there were three men in the boat: Kumm, 21 year old second cook Bernard Oberoski, of East Plymouth, Pennsylvania and Frank Tomczak of Buffalo, New York. Tomczak died of hypothermia about an hour before rescue. Oberoski

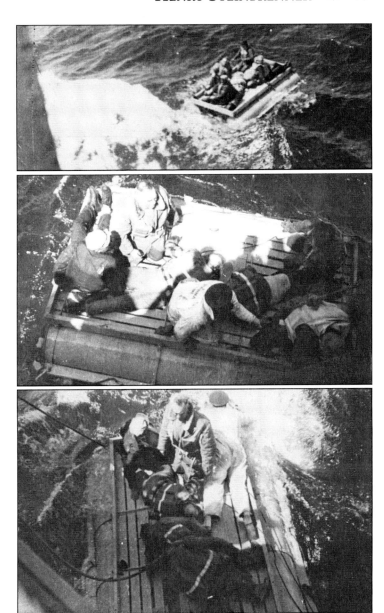

This sequence shows the rescue of the survivors from the liferaft by the Thompson. *Thro*

remembered, I was sucked down under and I don't know how long it was before I came up. I saw my life pass before me."[xxvi]

Captain Stiglin later reported, "We spent four hours on the raft. It bobbed up and down on top of the high waves. Spray flew over us, drenching our clothing. Once we saw one of the lifeboats bobbing in the water. The first mate lost consciousness on the raft. He died shortly after the rescue ship showed up." The mate was another victim of hypothermia.[xxvii]

The men on the life raft were terribly over crowded. Although he wasn't aboard Kumm remembers looking at the tiny raft with three other crewmen earlier on the trip and wondering how it could hold the number of men the Coast Guard claimed. The captain had earlier told them the raft was their best bet if anything happened.

Steinbrenner *survivors being rescued.*
Stonehouse Collection

*The dramatic rescue of seven men from the
lifeboat by the* D.M. Clemson. *Thro*

The *Joseph H. Thompson* rescued the men on the life raft and the *D. M. Clemson* picked up those on the starboard lifeboat (No. 2). Augsburger, who was on the lifeboat, remembered, "We huddled up in the sea anchor, that's what kept us alive. Another half hour and we would have been dead. He remembered the Coast Guard flew over but didn't see us."[xxviii]

As there are no atheists in foxholes, so are there none in lifeboats. Augsburger remembers he got more religion in four hours drifting around in the lifeboat than he could have received in four years in a seminary. The rescue by the *Clemson* seemed a miracle to him. "When I saw that big tin stack coming through the water it was beautiful."[xxix]

The *Clemson* missed them on the first pass and the lifeboat came dangerously near to the steamer's propeller. It would have been ironic had the seven men survived their long ordeal only to find death at a rescuers

Captain Everett of the Clemson *with some of the rescued men.* Augsburger

hands! On the second attempt Captain A. M. Everett of the *Clemson* was successful, laying her bulk such to provide a lee for the lifeboat, and one by one the frozen men were hauled aboard at the end of a manila rope. Once on deck the men were bundled off to the captain's cabin, given warm baths, hot food and dry clothing.[xxx]

Aboard the waterlogged port lifeboat, Kumm remembered that all that saved him and his companions was their size and weight. They were all "full size" men. Kumm thought he went from 225 pounds to 185 in four hours just shivering from the cold. There was nothing to bail the lifeboat out with but it didn't matter since the waves were washing into it quicker than the two half frozen men could have thrown it out. After an hour the two were numbed physically and mentally. At first they didn't dare move for fear of being washed out! Later they were so numbed they couldn't move.[xxxi] Once Tomczak's

The Sykes *provided a lee for the* Thompson *rescue.*
The photo is taken from the foredeck
of the Thompson. *Augsburger*

body washed overboard but Oberoski grabbed it and pulled it back aboard.

Captain George Fisher of the *Sykes* initially spotted the half flooded lifeboat when it pitched high on the crest of a wave. The lifeboat was pulled to the *Sykes* and a Jacob's ladder dropped. Kumm managed to grab it with the strength of a "death grip." The *Sykes* crew had to haul both the ladder and frozen Kumm aboard together. Before another man could follow Kumm, a swell whipped the lifeboat and the line snapped.

To make another try at saving the men Captain Fisher brought the massive *Sykes* around full circle which also cut down the sea. Although effective, the maneuver took nearly a full hour.

To complete the rescue, the third mate, Arthur Ritter and nine volunteers lowered the *Sykes* lifeboat and used it to bring the *Steinbrenner* boat in the steamer. The sea conditions were terrible and their action took a remarkably high degree of seamanship and a healthy dose of, in Mate Ritter's words later when praising his boat crew, "…plenty of guts."[xxxii]

Kumm remembered waking in the *Sykes* with two men rubbing his legs and trying to give him something to drink. When the ship arrived in Duluth both Kumm and Oberoski were taken to St. Mary's Hospital to recover from exposure, shock and bruising. Interviewed many years later, Kumm reminisced he rarely went swimming after his experience on Superior.[xxxiii]

The *Sykes* first learned of the *Steinbrenner* troubles when the first mate heard Stiglin's original radio call for help. At the time the *Sykes* was 35 miles distant. She and the *Thompson* arrived at the scene nearly simultaneously.

———————

The Canadian steamer *Ontadoc* of the N. M. Paterson fleet was upbound off Passage Island near the north tip of Isle Royale when she heard the *Steinbrenner* call for help. After contacting the downbound *Hochelaga*, the *Ontadoc* turned around and in tandem with the *Hochelaga* headed for the radioed position of the sinking ship; both vessels working their way down the east side of Isle Royale with the *Ontadoc* keeping well inside the larger *Hochelaga* for protection. As late arrivals to the scene they laid several miles off and stood by to render help as needed. Through binoculars the crewmen watched fascinated as the *Thompson*, *Clemson*, and *Sykes* went about their task of bringing the victims aboard. More vessels in the mix would have been dangerous although the *S.S. Curry* and *Sheadle* lay up wind and released oil smoothing the turbulent waters to aid in rescue. Later Captain W.A. Boult of the *Ontadoc* stated, "I wonder sometimes that they didn't turn over" and "those fellers really were using their heads. I don't know how they got those men aboard."[xxxiv] Not all made it. One

The U.S. Coast Guard buoy tender Woodrush *arrived on the scene from Duluth.* Stonehouse Collection

of the bodies was being hauled aboard when the lifejacket broke and it fell back into the water and disappeared. It was a grisly business.[xxxv]

Other carriers participating in the search were the *Imperial Leduc* and *Pathfinder*. The Coast Guard buoy tender *Woodrush* hurried over from Duluth. A Coast

36-foot Coast Guard Motor Lifeboats similar to this one also participated in the rescue. Stonehouse Collection

Guard lifeboat from Grand Marais, Minnesota was recalled due to the horrendous sea conditions. BM Paul Antalik, from Grand Marais claimed he, "had never seen the lake like that."[xxxvi] In the following days and weeks a total of ten bodies were recovered but seven remained missing. They remain missing to this day.

The 36-foot motor lifeboat from Portage Canal Coast Guard station under the command of BM1C John Mixon did punch through the storm arriving just before noon and managing to recover the remains of one lost sailor. Mixon apparently suffered a heart attack after he returned to the station due to the stress of the effort.[xxxvii]

Strangely, although advance warning had been given, some of the *Steinbrenner* crew appeared on deck without their life jackets. The third mate and his three men, trapped in the aft deckhouse and unable to reach their jackets stored in cabins forward, used jackets from the lifeboats. Many of the engine room gang also appeared without life jackets, since they were kept in their cabins on the weather deck. Since the deck was constantly swept by the seas, it was too dangerous to attempt to reach them. Nonetheless there clearly was panic as they could have grabbed the jackets kept in the engine room. In their haste to get topside, these were forgotten.[xxxviii]

Panic manifested itself in other ways. Oiler Augsburger remembered one of the men on the stern had enough sense to bring some blankets, but instead of throwing them into the lifeboat, he meaninglessly stuffed them down a ventilator.[xxxix]

Augsburger remembered there was nothing orderly about the evacuation. Panic stricken men were common.

In fact, one rare act of orderliness nearly cost the lifeboat crew their lives. It seems one of the men was ex-Coast Guard who, as the result of his years of training routinely secured the painter to the *Steinbrenner* rail. Thus when the boat was lowered and cast off from the falls, she was still secured to the sinking steamer! Since no one had a pocket knife to cut the rope, it appeared the lifeboat and all aboard would be pulled under by the *Steinbrenner*. By pure luck, the third assistant engineer, Arthur Morse of Michigan City, Indiana, appeared on deck and released the painter.[xl] Looking down at the men in the lifeboat he reportedly yelled, "You're on your own boys!" Morse made no effort to save himself, instead going down with the ship. His body was recovered several days later by the steamer *Clifford F. Hood*.[xli]

One of the engine room crew, Henry Johnson, kept his wits about him very well, but then he had a great deal of experience having been torpedoed twice by U-Boats in the Atlantic during World War II. When he received orders to abandon ship, he made certain to drop the throttle some to allow the *Steinbrenner* to "run away" from the lifeboats. It was an old trick he learned in the North Atlantic to put as much distance as possible between survivors and exploding boilers.[xlii]

In contrast with the panic aft, the forward end was calm and orderly due to the steady leadership of Captain Stilgin, a man well respected by this crew. Kumm remembered no panic among the men, that in the grip of the storm there was nothing that could be done and no time to do it. There was mostly pure shock at what was happening to them.[xliii]

When Captain Stiglin disembarked from the *Thompson* at the Soo, his terse statement concerning the loss was that,"the decks were awash and she was rolling and pitching. Three hatch covers were swept away and she filled with water." Captain Stiglin then went directly to the Objibwa Hotel to confer with company lawyers.[xliv] Losing a ship is always a nasty affair requiring the best of legal advice.

The dozen crewmen that disembarked at the Soo were treated decidedly shoddy, being hustled about more like cattle than men. Eventually each man submitted a detailed inventory of his processions lost when the ship sank. After the Coast Guard took their testimony, the company paid each man a $300 "sinking fee" but deducted the costs of new clothing needed to appear before the Coast Guard Board. The company wanted the men to look their best but didn't see why they should pay for it. The families of each of the men lost of course received the full $300, with no clothing deductions.

Worst of all was the fact many of the survivors left the *Steinbrenner* without enough money to buy a beer! The company made no effort to advance any money either. Luckily the good residents of the Soo took pity on the shipwrecked mariners and stood them to all the libation needed.[xlv]

The remaining survivors disembarked in Duluth where the treatment was much better. Kumm remembered having an excellent meal paid for by a citizen who took no thanks and remained anonymous.[xlvi]

The Coast Guard investigation began nearly as soon as the survivors arrived at the Soo. The investigators used the Federal building (the present River of History

Museum) as a base of operations. After taking relevant testimony from eleven of the crew, the Coast Guard cleared the room when Captain Stiglin testified. Questioned for hours, he related that all the navigational equipment was in working order except the radar. However it played no role in the sinking. Following his

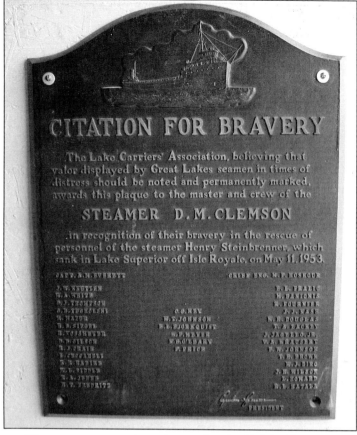

The commemorative plaque for the D.M. Clemson *presented by the Lake Carriers Association listed every crewmember.* Stonehouse Collection

appearance, the survivors, the Coast Guard board and the newspapermen covering the story all flew to Cleveland where the investigation wrapped up on May 18, a week after the loss. It was a remarkably quick job.[xlvii]

During the investigation some of the *Steinbrenner* crew were very critical of the 52 year old steamer. One of the watchmen claimed, "nothing worked as it should aboard the ship. We were taking water something awful for nearly 12 hours before she went down. For my money she just wasn't seaworthy!" He also indicated some of the stripped clamps were indeed on the aft three hatches, a point the Coast Guard Board of Investigation seemed to miss.[xlviii] Another crewman called her a "scow barge" while yet a third man said she was "just too old."[xlix]

But yet others said the old steamer was seaworthy. There was no question she was a "bucket," but Augsburger had sailed in her the year before and "had been through some good blows in her."[l]

The Inland Steel Company steamer *Wilfred Sykes* was honored by company officials for her part in the rescue of the two *Steinbrenner* crewmen from the lifeboat. At the time the *Sykes* was the flagship of the fleet and the holder of most of the speed and tonnage records on the Great Lakes. When she arrived at her dock at Indiana Harbor she was met by company dignitaries including the former president, Wilfred Sykes, the ship's namesake. Each officer and crewman was presented with a savings bond in recognition of the company's pride in the accomplishment. Sykes stated it was, "a remarkable feat of seamanship that the *Sykes* was even able to launch a small boat let alone rescue any of the men adrift." The operation was, "extremely hazardous" and "not only followed the tradition of the Lakes but performed heroically in the line of duty."[li]

The crews of all three Pittsburgh vessels were awarded gold medals by the Pittsburgh Steamship Company in recognition of their efforts. The following year the Lake Carriers Association presented each rescuing vessel with a large bronze plaque commemorating their teamwork and seamanship.[lii]

To the author's research, the Kinsman Transportation Company never formally acknowledged the assistance of any vessel, person, company or organization in the *Steinbrenner* disaster. The sooner it was forgotten, the better.

The *Steinbrenner* did not have the most illustrious career. In 1901 she launched prematurely at her Port Huron shipyard to avoid a dockyard fire. The old sailors always considered such an event to foretell an unlucky career. In the case of the *Steinbrenner* their fears were justified. On December 5, 1909 she collided with the steamer *Harry A. Berwind* just past Round Island in Mud Lake in the St. Marys River. The *Berwind's* bow hit the

The Steinbrenner *carrying a deck load of new autos.*
Marine Historical Society

The Steinbrenner *sunk in Mud Lake.* Thro

Steinbrenner midships tearing a 25-foot hole in her and sending her quickly to the bottom. Although her pilothouse was clear of the water and the stern cabin only half submerged, five feet of water covered her spar deck.

Famous Great Lakes salvor Tom Reid got the contract to raise her with a winning bid of $35,000. Since the

Salvaging the sunken steamer. Michigan State Archives

water was very murky during the sailing season and the channel ran right past the sunken *Steinbrenner*, Reid waited until shipping ended for the year and the river froze. His divers had a much easier time in the clearer water and not having to worry about a passing steamer was a real plus.

When the ice froze to a 12-inch thickness, the divers cut a hole through it, dropped down and went to work. Their

Locking down through the Soo Canal. Note she still has masts. Thro

Maneuvering in the Cuyahoga River. Rutherford B. Hayes

initial survey showed the *Steinbrenner*, which was filled with coal, actually sank deeper in the mud while Reid's crew waited for winter. The job was now much harder.

After clearing the mud away from the jagged hole in the hull, divers applied a timber "patch" and waited for spring. When the ice finally cleared they coffer dammed her hull and pumped her out. The coffer dam in effect extended her deck above water. The steamer floated free and the coffer dam removed. The salvage was completely successful and Reid turned a reported $10,000 profit.[liii]

In 1923 the *Steinbrenner* collided with the *John McCarthey* in Whitefish Bay. Combined damages totaled $15,000. The *Steinbrenner* damaged her port bow in October 1941 when she rammed a lock wall at the Soo;

$24,500 in yard work followed. Bad luck certainly wasn't a stranger to the *Steinbrenner*.

After probing the circumstances of the *Steinbrenner* loss, including interviewing all of the surviving crew, the Coast Guard Marine Board of Investigation concluded the "cause of the *Steinbrenner* foundering was heavy seas dislodging the three hatch covers, numbers 10, 11 and 12 and permitting flooding of the cargo holds. The adverse weather conditions with mountainous seas combined to make this foundering an "Act of God."[liv]

Without a doubt the Board felt the *Steinbrenner* was seaworthy as evidenced by the American Bureau of Shipping endorsement of the load line certificate and the issuance of her midsummer draft certificate on May 4, 1953. The steamer had been drydocked February 11-20, 1953 at Buffalo for her five-year survey for class and passed. She also passed her Coast Guard annual inspection. Captain Stiglin testified to the Board that when he was aboard earlier in the spring hauling grain, coal and running light, seas were taken aboard without experiencing any trouble.

The Board looked closely at the question of the stripped threads on the hatch clamps and concluded the news stories concerning them were greatly exaggerated. One of the survivors, Kenneth Kumm, testified that when wrapped with marlin they drew up as tightly as the others. Although the board considered Kumm short of sailing experience, they felt he was one of the most reliable and levelheaded men testifying.[lv]

There was never any testimony concerning the clamp threads on the aft three hatches, the hatches the Board concluded actually caused the foundering. No one ever claimed they were stripped, loose or otherwise unsecured.

How then did the hatch covers on hatches 10, 11 and 12 loosen and come free? The Board felt the working of the vessel in the heavy sea with metal clamps drawn tight on metal hatch covers, caused a general loosening of all the clamps. The heavy seas finished the job by knocking over the loosened clamps. Unsecured, the hatch covers came free. In the Board's opinion, the use of tarpaulins would have served to reduce the general working and loosening of the clamps and prevent the free entry of water between the hatch leaves.[lvi]

Strangely though, the Board did not blame Stiglin for failing to secure his hatches with the tarpaulins. They felt any reasonably prudent master under the same conditions considering the erroneous weather forecasts would have used the same judgment. Not battening down while underway was a case of an experienced seaman underestimating the force of the sea.[lvii]

The Board concluded the number two lifeboat was not properly launched due to panic. The crew realized the *Steinbrenner* was indeed sinking rapidly and no one was thinking too clearly. Contrary to the normal drill procedure, no man on the boat deck took charge of the lifeboat launching and confusion reigned.[lviii]

The Board formally recognized that the third assistant engineer, Arthur A. Morse's actions in releasing the painter for the number one lifeboat did save the lives of the seven men aboard it at the price of lessening his own chance for survival.[lix] During the investigation several crewmen testified that Morse assisted others into the lifeboat and then stayed aboard to cut a line forgotten by others. Morse perished with the ship. As the lifeboat drifted away, the engineer reportedly waved and said, "so long boys and good luck."

After deliberating the Board determined there was "no evidence that any licensed or certified personnel of the vessel committed any act of incompetence, inattention to duty or negligence of willful violation of any law or regulation. However the Board did feel the use of tarpaulins over the hatches would have prevented the casualty."[lx]

The Board recommended:

1. At least three life preservers carried in an overhead rack in the pilothouse.
2. At least four life preservers carried in the engine room.
3. At least six life preservers carried in a watertight box on the boat deck.
4. Tarpaulins required to be used on hatches at all times except the midsummer period of May 16 - September 15.
5. A letter of appreciation issued to the next of kin of the deceased third engineer.
6. Letters of congratulations be presented to the merchant vessels assisting.
7. The file on the *Steinbrenner* closed and no further action taken.[lxi]

But the Commandant of the Coast Guard reviewed the Board's investigation and disagreed, concluding the *Steinbrenner* was not lost to an "Act of God." Didn't the Board state that had the tarps been fitted over the hatches the *Steinbrenner* wouldn't have been lost? God had no business being blamed for human error.

Failure to fit the tarps was clearly against Coast Guard regulations. "It should be the responsibility of the master to assure himself before leaving protected waters that all exposed cargo hatches of his vessel are closed and made properly tight." Failure to comply with this regulation largely contributed to the vessels loss. Accordingly action was initiated against the license of the master.

The Commandant felt no further action was needed to require the fitting of tarps during certain periods. This was already stipulated in the previous regulation. The Commandant concluded no individual did anything beyond his duty and therefore a citation for a specific act of heroism for Morse was not warranted. He concurred with the recommendation concerning life preservers.[lxii]

And so ends the story of the loss of the steamer *Henry Steinbrenner* and the death of 17 of her crew. The reason for the sinking is not found in the easy excuse of fate, but rather in the simple fact that the ship had not been prepared to face the sea conditions encountered. Her hatch tarps had not been fitted and without them when the heavy weather struck the *Steinbrenner* was lost, while other vessels, more properly equipped, survived.

Footnotes

[i]*Evening News,* (Sault Ste. Marie, Michigan), May 31, 1953.
[ii]*Evening News*, May 31, 1953.
[iii]*Fort William Daily Times-Journal* (Ontario), May 13, 1953.
[iv]*Evening News*, May 31, 1953.
[v]*Fort William Daily Times-Journal*, May 31, 1953.
[vi]*Duluth News-Tribune*, May 12, 1953.
[vii]Marine Board of Investigation, Foundering of *SS Henry Steinbrenner*, May 11, 1953, U.S. Coast Guard.

[viii]*Fort William Daily Times-Journal*, May 31, 1953.

[ix]*Evening News*, May 31, 1953.

[x]Interview, Mr. Allen Augsburger, Valmy, WI, March 11, 1978.

[xi]*Duluth News Tribune*, May 11, 1953.

[xii]*Fort Williams Times-Journal*, May 13, 1953.

[xiii]Marine Board.

[xiv]*Evening News*, May 14, 1953.

[xv]*Soo Evening News*, May 13, 1953.

[xvi]*Annual Report, Lake Carriers Association*, 1953.

[xvii]Al Miller, *The Tin Stackers, The History of the Pittsburgh Steamship Company*, (Detroit: Wayne State University Press, 1999), pp. 180-182.

[xviii]Augsburger Interview.

[xix]*Duluth News-Tribune*, May 12, 1953.

[xx]*Soo Evening News*, May 12, 1953.

[xxi]Interview, Mr. Kenneth Kumm, Oxnard, CA. April 23, 1978.

[xxii] *Soo Evening News*, May 13, 1953.

[xxiii]*Milwaukee Journal*, May 11, 1953.

[xxiv]*Duluth News-Tribune*, May 14, 1953.

[xxv]Augsburger Interview.

[xxvi]*Soo Evening News*, May 19,1953.

[xxvii]*Fort Williams Daily Times-Journal*, May 13, 1953.

[xxviii]Augsburger Interview.

[xxix]Augsburger Interview.

[xxx]Miller, *Tin Stackers*, p. 181.

[xxxi]Kumm interview; Kumm correspondence, not dated.

[xxxii]*Duluth News Tribune*, May 12 1953.

[xxxiii]Kumm correspondence, not dated.

[xxxiv]*Fort William Daily Times-Journal*, May 12, 1953.

[xxxv]*Fort Williams Daily Times-Journal*, May 12, 1953.

[xxxvi]*Duluth News-Tribune*, May 12, 1953.

[xxxvii]Mac Frimodig, *Shipwrecks of the Keweenaw*, (Fort Wilkins Natural History Association, Michigan Department of Natural Resources, n.d.), p. 46.

[xxxviii]Augsburger Interview.

[xxxix]Augsburger Interview.

[xl]Augsburger, Interview; *Fort Williams Times-Journal*, May 12, 1953.

[xli]*Fort William Daily Times-Journal*, May 16, 1953.

[xlii]Augsburger Interview.

[xliii]Kumm Interview.

[xliv]*Soo Evening News*, May 12, 1953.

[xlv]Augsburger Interview.

[xlvi]Kumm Interview.

[xlvii]*Soo Evening News*, May 15, 1953.

[xlviii]*Soo Evening News*, May 15, 1953.

[xlix]*Soo Evening News*, May 15, 1953.

[l]Augsburger Interview.

[li]*Soo Evening News*, May 17, 1953.

[lii]Miller, *Tin Stackers*, p. 182,

[liii]Mary Francis Doner, *The Salvager,* (Minneapolis: Ross and Haines, 1958), P.

[liv]Marine Board.

[lv]Marine Board.

[lvi]Maine Board.

[lvii]Marine Board.

[lviii]Marine Board.

[lix]Marine Board.

[lx]Marine Board.

[lxi]Marine Board.

[lxii]Commandants Action, Marine Board.

✳ 5

PRINS WILLEM V

Lights, what lights? (Death of a Prince)
October 14, 1953

The proper display of a ship's lights is critical for safe navigation. Failure to show them or for another vessel to fail to see and understand them can have deadly results!

The whole mess started when the tug *Sinclair Chicago* left East Chicago at about 11:00 a.m. on October 13, 1954. The tug was pushing two barges, *Sinclair No. 11* carrying gasoline and *Sinclair No. 12* with heavy oil. All were bound for Milwaukee, 80 miles to the north. Enroute the weather turned foul and the tug brought her two charges into Waukegan for shelter, laying them up at the Hanna Coal Dock at 9:15 p.m. Waukegan was approximately a third of the way to Milwaukee. When the lake moderated the following morning, the tug took the *Sinclair No. 11* on to Milwaukee, reaching it at 9:02 a.m. on the 14th. Considering lake conditions, the captain thought it best to only haul one barge at a time. The tug then returned to Waukegan and took the *Sinclair No. 12* in tow, departing the harbor at 1:45 p.m. The barge was towed about 800 feet back behind the tug.

The *Sinclair Chicago*, 292 gross tons, 118.2 feet long with a 27.1-foot beam, was built in Wilmington, Delaware in 1926. Her twin diesels developed 1,900 horsepower, plenty of power for her job. Owned by Sinclair Refining and home ported in Chicago, she normally carried a crew of 16 men. The tank barge *Sinclair No. 12*, with a rated capacity of 12,500 gallons, was 193.8 feet in length and 35.9 feet in beam.

Having and displaying proper navigation lights on both tug and tow was critical. The type and arrangement was vital to let mariners know not only the direction they were proceeding, but also the type of vessel, in this case a tug pulling a barge.

In later testimony Captain Basetich of the *Sinclair Chicago* claimed portable sidelights were lashed to the forward bitts of the barge when the tow was made up in Waukegan. The sidelights were complete units with lamps and batteries in waterproof cases. Normally the sidelights would have been mounted on pipe stands about six feet off the deck, however, since the stands were missing, he just lashed them to the low bitts. He also claimed both port and starboard lights on the barge were on and working when the tug left the dock. The lights on the tug were also on as verified by the distribution panel. When a bulb was out or light not working, a tell-tale illuminated and a buzzer sounded. Since the panel in the pilothouse was lighted correctly and silent, all was well. Besides her normal red and green sidelights she showed several other lights because the tug was towing, including: a masthead (20 points) about her deckhouse, a range light (32 points) above and behind the deckhouse, a towing light (20 points) above the masthead light, and various deck lights. Seeing the light arrangement would alert another vessel it was a tug and she had a tow, so keep a sharp watch.

When the tow cleared the Outer Buoy she swung around to a course of 331 degrees true for Milwaukee. Speed was about 8.4 mph, which was full throttle. Although the weather was cloudy, visibility was good. The wind was blowing west northwest and strong with a northwest chop but presented no danger. Approaching Milwaukee the city's lights were clearly visible. All in all it wasn't a bad night on the lake for the middle of October.

Meanwhile the Dutch motor vessel *Prins Willem V* enters the scene. She began her trip to the Lakes from the Netherlands and stopped at a number of ports before finally reaching Milwaukee with a cargo of general freight. After discharging cargo she loaded general freight including wet salted cowhides, horsetail hair, cattle tails, dried peas, sausage casings, machinery, hog casings, Wurlitzer jukeboxes, salted fat backs, television picture tubes, and other merchandise, then departed the Municipal Transit Shell Dock at 6:29 p.m. heading back out into Lake Michigan, bound for Sarnia on Lake Huron and an eventual return home. While all navigation lights were on, her radar wasn't. Radar was still a relatively new piece of equipment and many masters only used it when visibility was very poor. Who would need it on such a nice night on Lake Michigan?

The *Prins Willem*, registered in the Netherlands with a homeport of Rotterdam, was an ocean freighter owned by the Mij Zeetransport, N.V, (Oranje Line). A typical small freighter of 1,567 gross tons, she was 258 feet long, diesel powered with a single crew. There were two cargo holds

The Prins Willem V unloading. Note the cargo booms in the up position. Stonehouse Collection

with the deckhouse and engine room between them. The *Prins Willem* had an unusual history. Built in 1940 she was scuttled in the Nieuwe Waterweg near Maasluis, Netherlands to both block the canal and prevent the Germans from using her. Raised in 1947, she was refurbished and returned to service a year later.

Approaching Milwaukee at 7:05 p.m., about two hours after sunset, the tug turned to 305 degrees true to head northward of the Milwaukee breakwater entrance. Once she closed up the entrance she would shorten the tow for better control then run on into the harbor. Everything was normal. The pilothouse was well manned; the captain conning the tug, the relief master, wheeling her, a lookout and a deck watchman on duty. In later testimony all claim they clearly saw the barge's running lights only moments before the fatal collision.

At the same time the *Prins Willem* was passing out through the breakwater entrance on a course of due east at 12 knots, full speed for the small freighter. She was heading for the designed Lake Carrier's Association point of departure for courses out of the city, about two and a half miles ahead. When the *Prins Willem* reached the departure point she planned to turn northeastward for Point Betsie on the Michigan shore. It was all very routine. On clearing the entrance the Canadian pilot, Mr. Wright, placed her on automatic pilot and went below, turning the ship over to the third mate. Several minutes later the second mate, Mr. Van Den Bergh relieved the watch and the third mate went below but before leaving the bridge told the second mate he had sighted the lights of a vessel on the starboard bow. The master, Pierre J. A.

Huilmand, was also still on the bridge. Strangely there was no lookout or regular wheelsman. The captain was acting as the lookout. No lookout was on the bow either.

Ten minutes after 7:00 p.m., the second mate took a sighting on the lights off the starboard bow, determining a bearing of 120 degrees true and about two miles away. Both master and mate looked at the stranger with their binoculars and seeing her red sidelight determined that a port to port crossing was in order and by the rules of the road, he was required to alter course to allow the stranger to safely cross his path. Neither man saw any lights indicating a tow.

Two minutes later the mate took another sighting, indicating the bearing was roughly the same and distance had decreased to a mile. The captain ordered the mate to swing right to 140 degrees true, a change of 50 degrees, to allow *Prins Willem* to stay well clear of the crossing vessel. The mate turned off the automatic pilot and hand

The Dutch freighter Prins Willem *was a frequent visitor to the Great Lakes. Stonehouse Collection*

wheeled her to the new course. No whistle signal indicating a course change was blown.

When the bearing of the tug was about 5 points off the port bow of the *Prins Willem*, the captain instructed the mate to swing her slowly left to pass safely clear of the tug's stern. The vessels were now less than a half-mile apart. Captain Huilmand went out on the starboard bridge wing and looked closely at the tug but saw nothing to indicate a barge was astern. She was just a tug proceeding on her way. Nothing to be unduly concerned about. The side lights were the key. The deck of the barge was only about three feet above the water. Without the lights she was invisible, hidden in the gloom of the lake!

The pilothouse crew on the tug had only just sighted the *Prins Willem* red sidelight. Considering the tremendous number and variety of lights from the city, it is easy to understand how the *Prins Willem* lights could have been lost in the riot of illumination. Captain Basetich mentioned to the relief captain that the *Prins Willem* must be a foreign ship or a Coast Guard vessel since no security call was heard on channel 51 on the ship-to-shore radio-telephone. Security calls are informal declarations of vessel movements and intentions. For example, when the *Prins Willem* pulled away from her dock she would have broadcast the action and her plan to go through the breakwater entrance. It was a very informal but effective method of traffic control. However neither salties or Coast Guard cutters were in the habit of using it.

Like the freighter, the tug didn't sound a whistle signal. However as a safety measure, the captain turned on his big carbon arc spot light and aimed it at the barge as a warning. The tug captain watched in horror as the

Prins Willem turned, clearly intending to run between the tug and barge. Immediately the tug's captain sounded five short whistle blasts, the traditional Great Lakes danger signal and swung the search light from the barge to the freighter and back again. When the freighter didn't change course the captain stopped his engines and sent a man running to the stern to slack the towline from the towing engine. Captain Basetich figured if he slacked the towline from 800 to 1500 feet it should drop to the bottom and with luck the freighter could slip over it when it ran between the tug and barge.

Basetich's luck was all bad. At 7:16 p.m. the starboard bow of the barge slammed into the starboard side of the *Prins Willem* just abreast of hatch number two of the number one cargo hold forward of the forward engine room bulkhead, holing the *Prins Willem* severely. One source estimated the hole was twenty feet by eight feet! That works out to a 160-square foot hole! The two vessels hit at roughly a 50-degree angle, bounced apart briefly but the barge swung back into the *Prins Willem*, smashing another hole roughly two feet by fifteen feet running fore and aft opposite the engine room compartment. The result was an additional 30 square feet of hole. The two vessels slid apart in the dark night.

Interviewed later the men in the pilothouse of the *Prins Willem* claimed it was only when the tug turned on the search light that they realized something was seriously wrong. They never heard the frantic whistle blasts or saw any navigation lights on the barge. Finally seeing the danger, the captain of the *Prins Willem* threw the rudder hard over in an effort to minimize damage by swinging into rough course alignment with the other vessel. He did

The Dutchman's crew was well disciplined and professional. Stonehouse Collection

not slacken speed or sound a whistle signal. The actual collision happened about 1.7 miles east of the breakwater entrance. The impact was easy enough no one on the *Prins Willem* was knocked off their feet. For the men not in the pilothouse it was more of a, "what the hell was that?"

None of the men on the tug heard the collision or felt it reverberate through the steel cable. Looking back at the barge with binoculars they plainly saw the smashed bow; stark evidence of what happened. Ominously the sidelights were not burning. Quickly Captain Basetich called the Coast Guard, notifying them of the disaster. He also started to haul in the towline to bring the barge up to the tug. He didn't want to drop the cable and leave an unlit barge loaded with oil drifting around loose in the middle of the traffic lane.

Aboard the *Prins Willem* things were going from bad to worse very quickly. Water immediately flooded into cargo hold number one and the vessel quickly listed to starboard. Both engine rooms were also flooding at an alarming rate and the engines soon stopped. Without the

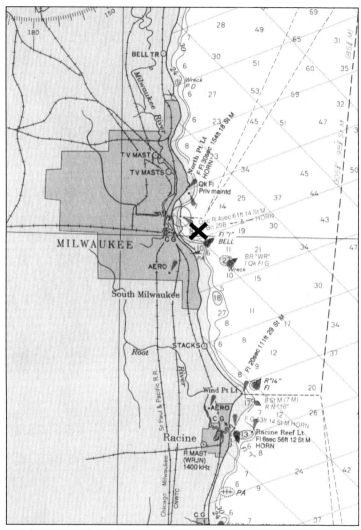

engines running, the pumps could not run. They were just so much junk steel. At least the auxiliary generator ran for about half an hour providing some illumination for the dying freighter. After a quick inspection of the damage the first mate and chief engineer told the captain she was lost. At 7:30 p.m. a reluctant MAYDAY call was made and preparations for abandoning ship started.

The Coast Guard at nearby McKinley Beach was a little ahead of the curve. A sharp-eyed lookout spotted the 7:15 p.m. searchlight and reported it only moments before the call from the tug came in. At 7:18 p.m. motor rescue boat 30376 pulled away from the dock followed quickly by motor lifeboat 36505. The big 180-foot buoy tender *Hollyhock* left the dock a little after 8:00 p.m. to lend her assistance. All in all, it was a remarkably fast response by the Coast Guard!

Regardless of how fast the Coast Guard was coming aboard the *Prins Willem* time was very short and the captain ordered his men off. The two lifeboats were lowered smartly and the crew abandoned her, 22 in the low side boat and six in the high side boat. None of the crew was injured in the collision or in abandoning ship. The freighter was soon listing between 55 and 60 degrees, just hanging on her side. The captain and radio operator stayed aboard until the Coast Guard picket boat arrived, defying the ship to sink beneath them. When the Coast Guard boat laid-up to the rail, they both deftly stepped from the freighter into the boat. Within minutes of their leaving her, the freighter dove for the bottom.

The buoy tender *Hollyhock* picked up both lifeboats and brought the survivors back to Milwaukee where they were put up at the Pfister Hotel. Shipwreck sailors deserved the best!

While the *Prins Willem* was sinking the tug was busy. By 7:58 p.m. she had had her barge hauled-up alongside and the crew examined the extensive damage. The barge was down by the head, which was now nearly awash and the bow was smashed back about six feet. When the crew went aboard to cast off the towline (so they could make up a side tow), they noticed the sidelights from both sides were missing. What had happened to them? There was no evidence of their somehow being knocked off in the collision. The damage didn't go that far back. Were they ever there to begin with?

The *Prins Willem* gave up and dove bow first for the bottom at 8:22 p.m. She was approximately three and three-quarters miles, due east of the breakwater entrance. After due evaluation the freighter was abandoned by the owners and declared a total loss of $1,250,000. The cargo was an additional loss of $750,000. Injury to the barge was estimated at $15,000.

There was of course the inevitable Coast Guard investigation. Their experts listened to the testimony of both crews, examined the various logs and official documents and looked closely at the damage to the barge. They reached a number of conclusions:

1. There was no evidence sidelights were ever placed on the barge regardless of the captain's claims they were. Had they been on the barge and knocked off by the collision, there had to be something left behind, perhaps a piece of rope or even a scrape on the hull. The bitts were not damaged and the hull of the freighter did not hit anywhere near the area. When closely questioned as to how he secured the lights, the captain's answers did match the bitts on the barge. In effect they felt he couldn't have tied the lights off as he claimed. The log of the tug showed it only took 15 minutes to ready the tow

for sea. The Coast Guard felt this was too little time to accomplish everything needing to be done. Were the sidelights left off with the press of time?

2. Although the *Sinclair Chicago* was displaying the proper number of lights to indicate a tow, they were improperly displayed. As a result, when the captain of the *Prins Willem* saw her, he failed to realize she had a barge astern. The two lights on the foremast of the tug were spaced too close together. Great Lakes pilot rules called for them to be in a vertical line not less than six feet apart. The lights on the *Sinclair Chicago* were only two feet, six inches apart and the lower light was nearly a foot off-set from the vertical. The lower light was also set so low, it looked to be a deck light instead of a proper navigation signal.

3. The *Prins Willem* also received an admonition. When the captain ordered the freighter to starboard to swing around the tug, he should have sounded a whistle signal as required by the pilot rules. Having heard the signal, the tug was bound by the rules to reply either with the same signal indicating approval, or the danger signal if she deemed the intended action unsafe. Although the *Prins Willem* captain complained it was too noisy on his bridge to hear a whistle signal, the rules still required it.

4. A proper watch was not kept on the *Prins Willem*. While the captain's position on the

bridge is certainly a good thing, he can't do the jobs of captain and lookout at the same time. As master his duties clearly conflict with those of a lookout. Not only did he order the various course changes, he also kept the log indicating the time the courses were changed, noted the various bearings taken, took reports from the mate, etc. He was not able to keep the tug under close observation as a dedicated lookout would have nor was he stationed in the lookout position on the bow. The only other man in the pilothouse was the mate and since he was wheeling, he couldn't properly act as lookout either. In effect the *Prins Willem* was running in congested waters without a proper lookout, contrary to Pilot Rules.

5. The problems of the lack of a lookout and confusing/lack of lights on the tug and barge not withstanding, the captain of the *Prins Willem* took the right actions to safely pass astern of the *Sinclair Chicago* had it not been for the unlit barge. When the captain realized the barge was there, it was too late for any effective action.

6. The investigators felt the pilot should not have left the bridge while she was still in congested waters. Clearly his expertise could have been valuable to the *Prins Willem* crew.

7. The Coast Guard believed the tug's captain made a good decision when he slacked his tow cable in a effort to let the freighter cross without fouling it. He made another good decision when he didn't abandon the lightless barge after the collision.

8. It was clear the use of normal security calls could have prevented the accident. Had a simple radio call been made, most likely nothing untoward would have happened.

9. Likewise had the *Prins Willem* used her radar, the barge would have been seen and master could have swung safely behind her.

10. The Board recommended the owners of the *Sinclair Chicago* be cited for failure to display proper towing signals. There was considerable confusion whether any action could be taken against the captain of the *Prins Willem* as she was a foreign vessel. Without any other real options, the Coast Guard forwarded a copy of their investigation to the Dutch government for their action as they thought appropriate. The disaster did cause the Coast Guard to begin to examine the problem of assuring competent officers aboard the increasing number of saltwater vessels entering the Great Lakes. It would be a growing problem when the St. Lawrence Seaway opened in the near future, allowing a flood of foreign ships into the Great Lakes.[i]

Prins Willem was not a unique Oranje Line visitor to the Lakes. Over the years a total of 24 of the company's ships traded on the Inland Seas. Most of them stayed out of trouble, but not always. The *Prins Alexander* collided with the *Silver Isle* near Kingston, Ontario in June 1963. Neither vessel was lost.

On instruction of the owner, the Roen Steamship Company examined the wreck shortly after the sinking to determine the potential for salvage. Roen discovered her laying on her port side in about 75 feet of water with 33 feet over her port side rail. Roen offered to raise her for $268,000 on a "no cure, no pay" basis but the company declined the offer. Some of the cargo was salvaged but much was left in place.

Reportedly the Oranje Line sued Sinclair for $2 million. It was settled out of court for a rumored $200,000 plus payment by Sinclair. Oranje Line of course collected it's insurance from Lloyd's of London and turned the wreck over the U.S. Army Corps of Engineers. Since the wreck extended relatively close to the surface thus presenting a hazard to navigation, the Corps in turn awarded a bid to a Milwaukee diver backed by a syndicate of Milwaukee businessmen for $50,000 to clear the wreck to a safe 40-foot depth. The group was given 180 days to do the job and once it was successfully accomplished, they were to receive title to the wreck. As required, the syndicate posted a $440,000 performance bond. However as time passed and the diver did no work, the syndicate

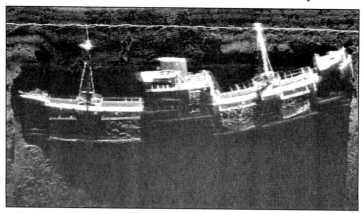

Captain Jerry Guyer from Len-Der Charters, 900 kHz-side scan using Marine Sonic Technology equipment.

members became very nervous, seeing the bond being forfeit. Feeling the pressure the syndicate members turned over their interest in the wreck to the diver to encourage him to get busy and dynamite the wreck as their contract stipulated. Regardless of what the motivation was, the diver finally went out and did the job. It was disgustingly easy which angered the syndicate members, feeling they had been fooled into giving up their interests. All the diver did was cut away a gangway and a door, the only portions actually projecting above the 40-foot level! Reportedly it took a mere 20 minutes of work! The Corps was angry too, feeling that they also got "took." But in the end they paid the diver $46,000 as stipulated.

The first major effort to raise the *Prins Willem* was in 1958 by the original "cutting diver." Four 50-foot long, ten foot diameter, steel pontoons were secured to the wreck with steel cables. In theory air would be pumped into the pontoons and the wreck would magically rise to the surface of Lake Michigan. During the night of September 25 however, while air was being pumped into the pontoons for the first time , one of the monsters broke loose, rocketing to the surface like a Poseidon missile from a submerged nuclear submarine. As failures go, it wasn't much but it did bankrupt the salvage company. Although the original diver and his wife died in a traffic accident in 1960, their rights passed to another consortium salvage in 1961. The new group intended to use 42 parachute bags to try to "lift" the wreck. It failed too. The rights were eventually sold at auction for $85,000 to an Illinois businessman planning to use is as kind of a floating sales office for fire prevention equipment. As with previous salvage efforts, it was just a pipe dream.

A diver explores the wreck. Ric Mixter

The *Prins Willem* is proving to be an attractive although dangerous wreck for divers. At this writing four divers have been killed exploring her; the first in 1985, second in 1989, third in 1992 and fourth in 1997. At 70 feet or so, the wreck is not especially deep but she is relatively intact and visibility is often poor. Getting lost or disoriented can lead to an early demise for an unwary diver.[ii]

Divers have recovered a number of artifacts from the wreck, including a 10-ton spare "bucket" or propeller blade. Several tons of printing presses, cartons of salted fatbacks, table silver from the mess and other items have been carried away by underwater salvagers. One enterprising group blew the propeller off with dynamite. It is now on display at the Lower Lakes Marina in Milwaukee. Today the "Willie" as she is commonly called, is one of the most popular dive sites in Lake Michigan.

Footnotes

[i]Marine Board of Investigation: Collision, M./V *Prins Willem V* (Netherlands) and Barge *Sinclair No. 12*, under tow, Lake Michigan, 14 October 1954; Telescope, September-October, 1981, p. 118, 121; John H. Purves, *Roen Steamship Company, The Way It Was, 1909-1946*, pp. 67-68; *Milwaukee Journal*, October 12, 1984.

[ii]Frederick Stonehouse, *Haunted Lakes, More Great Lakes Ghost Stories*, Duluth, Lake Superior Port Cities, 2000, pp. 97-99.

✳ 6

MONROVIA &
ROYALTON
Out of the fog.
June 25, 1959

When the *Prins Willem* and *Sinclair No. 12* collided off Milwaukee Harbor, the congested waters played a part in the mishap, as did the failure to display proper lights, use radar, radio or correct whistle signals. To a greater or lesser degree, radar, radio and sound signals all played a role in the *Monrovia - Royalton* collision on Lake Huron too. The collision was also the first major shipping accident in the Great Lakes since the opening of the St. Lawrence Seaway. The last major disaster was the loss of the *Carl D. Bradley* on Lake Michigan on November 18, 1958.

The 6,674 gross ton *Monrovia*, Liberian registry, was as a dry-cargo freighter built by Lithgrows Ltd., Glasgow, Scotland in 1943. Originally named *Empire Falstaff*, she had a length of 447 feet and beam of 56 feet and powered by a single triple expansion steam engine. Being registered in a country like Liberia is often called a "flag of convenience." Shipping rules concerning safety, insurance, crew training and operational standards, etc. are very lax in such third world countries,

The Liberian freighter Monrovia was a stranger on the Great Lakes. Stonehouse Collection

so it is far cheaper to register ships there than it is in more reputable nations like the U.S., Canada, Britain, Norway, etc. Today the top six flag of convenience "nations" in terms of tonnage registered are Panama, Liberia, Bahamas, Greece, Cyprus and Malta. The ships never actually "visit" these countries. They just serve as legal points of registry for corporate business. Using such flags of convenience is one of the "dirty little secrets" the maritime industry, in 1959 as well as today.

The *Royalton*, Canadian registry, was a 7,164 gross ton, Great Lakes bulk freighter owned and operated by the Scott Misener Steamships of Port Colborne, Ontario. The 536-foot vessel was built by Collingwood Shipbuilding Company in 1924. For a time she sailed as the flagship of the A. E. Mathews fleet. When the company went out of business in 1932 during the depths of the Depression, she was taken over by Toronto Elevators but spent most of her time moored to a dock. Cargoes of any kind were rare. In 1933 she was acquired the Colonial Steamship Company, later to be known as Scott Misener Steamships. Although times were tough, at least she was sailing. Typical cargoes included iron, grain and coal, from wherever to wherever as needed. Shipping companies were not choosy during the Depression.

During her career, the *Royalton* had a couple of scrapes with danger. On May 6, 1934 she assisted the freighter *Ten* on Lake Superior when she suffered a catastrophic engine breakdown. On June 6, 1958 she damaged her bow in a collision with the canaller *William C. Warren* in the Welland Canal. The *Royalton* was finally scraped at La Spezia, Spain in 1980-81.

The Royalton was built in 1924. Stonehouse Collection

First lets look at the disaster from the standpoint of the salty. The *Monrovia* dropped her Canadian pilot at the Lake Huron Lightship shortly before 2:15 a.m. on June 25, 1959. Once the pilot was clear, she came to a course of 353 degrees true and rang up 55 revolutions giving her a speed of nine miles an hour. She was bound from Montreal for Chicago and Duluth with a cargo of 4,000 tons of sheet and bar steel. The cargo was originally loaded in Antwerp, Belgium. Her master, a Greek national named Stefanos Svokos, was on the bridge and would remain so until the fatal collision, as were the first and second mates. The *Monrovia* did not have radar, which was unusual for the times, as most commercial vessels were so equipped. The captain also did not post a lookout on the bow as was commonly done. Given the lack of radar, a lookout would have seemed very "prudent."

At 4:30 a.m. visibility decreased greatly and the big whistle started blowing the required fog signals. When the ship passed Harbor Beach the light was unseen in the gray fog but the fog signal clearly heard. The captain came left to 344 degrees true and continued on. Speed was not reduced regardless of the thick fog. At noon the captain estimated he was off Thunder Bay Island based on a single Radio Direction Finder (RDF) bearing, the taffrail log and a depth finder reading. He altered course to 340 degrees true and reduced speed to 50 revolutions, or 8 miles per hour. At the time RDF was considered reasonably high technology but it was no substitute for radar.

An hour and a half later after the radio operator took another RDF bearing on Thunder Bay Island Light and depth finder reading the captain was convinced it was time to change course to 020 degrees true to swing well clear of the Thunder Bay Island reefs. About five minutes later the captain heard the mournful whistle blasts from a nearby vessel. The sound seemed to be from dead ahead to slightly on the port bow. As the *Monrovia* continued on into the gray mist the signals continued to be heard from the same general area. Ominously they also grew louder! About 1:54 p.m. the captain blew a single blast on his whistle for a port-to-port passing and ordered his rudder hard over to the right. No answering whistle was heard but the fog signals continued to blow. The stranger should have replied with one blast, indicating I heard you and agree with your plan. This <u>assumes</u> the stranger heard the signal! Three minutes later the *Monrovia's* captain blew another single blast, again for a port-to-port crossing. A couple of minutes passed and the huge bow of a steamer materialized out of the fog just ahead at an angle of 60 to 90 degrees. The stranger's bow bit deep into the *Monrovia* striking her just behind the bridge!

Now switch to the *Royalton* downbound from Duluth to Montreal with a full cargo of 10,670 tons of grain. After an uneventful run down Lake Superior, through the Soo Locks and down the St. Marys River, she passed Detour Reef Light (at the northern end of Lake Huron) at 6:15 a.m. on June 25. The second mate, Edmond Langstaffe had the con. On reaching the open lake she increased speed to full ahead, 11.4 miles per hour. About 11:45 a.m. fog set in and her whistle began to blow the standard fog signals. As normal procedure, a lookout was sent to the bow and the speed reduced to 11.2 mph. The captain now took the con. The front centerline pilothouse window was opened and the captain took station behind it. While the lookout was expected to report whatever he heard, the captain wanted to be in position to hear and see too!

At 1:05 p.m. Thunder Bay Light was marked on the radar as 9.6 miles off the starboard beam. An RDF bearing also confirmed the direction. The captain changed course to 159 degrees true and 15 minutes later sighted a radar target 13 miles ahead and slightly on the starboard bow. To stay well clear of the unknown vessel the *Royalton* swung five degrees left and held the new course for 12 to 15 minutes and left again five degrees for another eight to ten minutes. The target was now ten miles away and both captain and mate assumed they would pass starboard to starboard with at least a mile separation. At 1:40 p.m. the unknown target was bearing 30 to 35 degrees on the starboard and five miles distant. Again the *Royalton* course was changed 12 degrees to the left, steadying up on 137 degrees true. Both captain and mate kept a sharp eye on the radar showing the strange ships movements. The *Royalton's* speed also decreased to 3 mph. The men in the pilothouse now heard a three-blast fog signal for the first time. It was about 30 degrees on the starboard bow right where the radar indicated the target was located. He must have thought, "Damn it! Whoever you are, just go away. Stop turning into me!"

Earlier the mate had over heard radio traffic indicating a salty was upbound but running in the downbound shipping lane. He relayed the information to the captain who tried to call the strange ship on channel 51. "Salt water ship upbound on the downbound course." He tried the call three times but received no response. They were close enough he could almost have yelled! He was sure it was the same ship he was seeing on his radar. Why wasn't the upbound vessel answering the radio call?

When the two ships were about four miles apart the *Royalton* sounded two blasts, indicating she was planning a starboard-to-starboard passing. No reply was heard so when they were two and half to three miles distant she repeated the two-blast signal. The reply was a single blast. What did the strange ship think she was doing? Immediately the *Royalton* captain sounded the danger signal and rang full astern followed by emergency full astern! Thirty seconds later the bow of the *Monrovia* loomed out of the fog 400 feet away about 45 degrees on the starboard bow, and swinging hard right. At 1:57 she collided with the *Royalton* which was dead in the water or with slight stern movement because of the full astern engine.

After the collision, the *Royalton* stood by to assist but the fog soon hid the *Monrovia* from sight. Damage to the *Royalton* was limited to the extreme end of the bow smashed in and a flooded forepeak. She was in no danger and assistance was not needed.

The *Monrovia* was a different story. Reading the official reports gives the clear but unstated message that panic reigned aboard the salty! Immediately after the impact, the captain of the *Monrovia* ordered the engineers to start pumping number two hold, the area where the *Royalton's* bow sliced into the freighter. The engineer on watch quickly opened the ballast suction line valves as needed but before he could start the pumps he was called on deck to abandon ship. No other officer, deck or engineer went into the lower engineer room to access damages or take action to save the ship. Instead, everyone ran for the lifeboats! This clearly was not a well trained or disciplined crew.

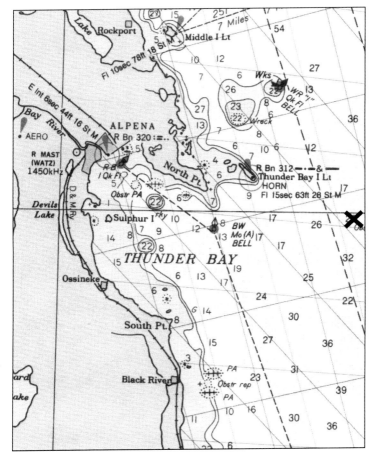

Since the *Monrovia* had not held a lifeboat drill in a very long time, no one was sure how the boats were prepared or lowered. After an hour of "Keystone Cop" confusion the 29 man crew successfully abandoned her in a single lifeboat and ended up bobbing happily around on foggy Lake Huron. In the panic to desert the ship she was left in slow ahead with the engines still running. The dying ship continued to move through the fog, like a ghost ship not yet buried. In the meantime the steamer *Norman S. Foy* arrived and recovered the frightened crew. None were injured. The 552-foot *Foy* was downbound about 15 minutes behind the *Royalton* when the pilothouse crew noticed on radar the two vessels stopped close together. Learning of the collision, Captain Alex Gillies steamed in to lend assistance. When her help was no longer needed she continued down, dropping the crew at Detroit. The *Foy* was owned by the Browning Steamship Company of Detroit.

After a while the captain of the *Monrovia* became concerned his ship wasn't sinking fast enough. After all, when a captain orders abandon ship, it is assumed the ship is sinking and effective action to save her is not possible. For the ship not to sink is a great embarrassment. Apparently in an effort to see why his sinking ship wasn't sinking, the captain, first and second officers and two engineers boarded her. When they discovered water in the number 2 and 3 holds as well as machinery spaces they decided nothing could be done to save the ship so they recovered their personal gear and returned to the *Foy*. As the *Monrovia* still refused to sink, a second trip recovered additional crew belongings was made. Strangely there was no effort to save the logs books or charts, critical evidence of the ship's last movements. Not having access to this vital evidence proved a hindrance for the investigators in determining what actually happened on the bridge during the crucial time before the impact with the *Royalton*. This leads to the inevitable question of whether they were deliberately left? Was it to the benefit of the officers <u>not</u> to have such official records available? Left to die, the *Monrovia* slowly flooded. Ten minutes after midnight, over eight hours after the collision, the *Monrovia*, listing to the port, sank by the head in 150 feet of water. All that remained was a huge pile of debris floating on the fog-shrouded waves.

It is hard to comprehend that throughout more than ten hours the *Monrovia* floated after the collision, the captain did nothing to save his ship! He certainly did add to the reputation of the Greek maritime community.

The Royalton *sported a smashed bow after colliding with the* Monrovia. *Stonehouse Collection*

Several Coast Guard vessels assisted in the episode. Icebreaker *Mackinaw* arrived on scene at 2:30 a.m. on the 26th and buoy tender *Acacia* a little more than an hour later. *Acacia* marked the wreck site with a buoy. Coast Guard Air Station Traverse City, Michigan sent three planes to the area but the fog prevented their effective assistance. Various small craft were initially dispatched but were recalled when it was clear they weren't needed. The 25-foot launch from Middle Island Light made it to the scene before being sent back to the station. On the return it was forced to stop at Thunder Bay Island Station when it got lost in the fog.

When word of the collision reached shore, two Coast Guardsmen in another 25-foot launch went out to assist. Lightkeeper Allen Kane and Boatswain's Mate 3rd class David Brock departed the Alpena Light Station at 3:00 p.m. while the fog was still thick. When their radio failed the two were out of touch with either ship or shore and as

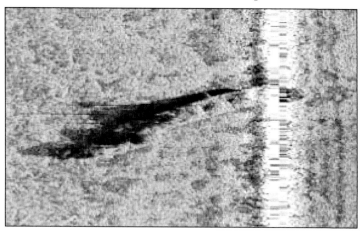

A side scan sonar image of the Monrovia. *The wreck is a popular diving target.* Stonehouse Collection

a result, the Coast Guard started a search with ships and aircraft to rescue the rescuers. Both wives waited anxiously at the station for news of their husbands. At noon the next day they were spotted about three miles off Thunder Bay Island. Two civilian boats also headed for the scene, the 34-foot *Marjoe* and an 18-foot *Sea Skiff*. Both returned before reaching the scene when it was apparent all was under control.

This was the first trip to the Great Lakes for the *Monrovia* and her officers were grossly unprepared for it. Their only knowledge of Great Lakes Pilot Rules and courses came from publications and charts they picked up in Montreal on June 16. Only the master and radio operator could speak, read or understand English and then only at the most questionable level. The *Monrovia* was clearly an accident waiting to happen.

A Coast Guard Board of Investigation looked at the data, took testimony from all concerned and issued a number of conclusions:

1. The cause of the collision was the failure of the *Monrovia* to reduce speed to a bare minimum and navigate with caution when she heard the fog signal of the *Royalton*, apparently dead ahead.

2. Both vessels were out of the tracks recommended by the Lake Carriers Association and Dominion Marine Corporation. While not the cause, it was a factor in the collision. However the Coast Guard did note that the east limits of the upbound track between Middle Island Light and Thunder Bay Island Light are drawn such to force a ship to pass very close to

a 22-foot shoal. Although marked with a lighted bell buoy, it was a significant hazard for a deeply laden vessel like the *Monrovia*, which was drawing 19.3 feet. Her swing around this point and into the downbound track was understandable. If she carried a Great Lakes pilot, he likely would have done the same, especially considering navigation was by RDF and depth finder, not radar.

3. The Board also thought if the *Monrovia* had a bow lookout he might have heard the *Royalton's* whistles sooner, thus avoiding the collision.

4. The *Monrovia* should have sounded the danger signal when she didn't get a response to her original single whistle signal. This was a rule violation but since the *Royalton* was already taking evasive action, it likely would not have avoided the collision.

5. The *Monrovia* was cited for failing to slow to bare steerageway when she heard the *Royalton* fog signal for failing to sound the danger signal.[i]

The *Monrovia* is a popular target for Lake Huron divers. She is reported largely upright with depths of 125-140 feet.

Footnotes

[i]Marine Board of Investigation; collision between the *SS Monrovia* (Liberian) and the *SS Royalton* (Canadian), Lake Huron, 25 June 1959; *The Alpena News*, June 26-27, 1959; Rev. Peter Van der Linden, ed. *Great Lakes Ships We Remember II*, (Cleveland: Freshwater Press, n.d.), p. 338.

CARL D. BRADLEY

An explosion of flame and smoke.
November 18, 1958

A strong gale was blowing as the 254-foot German motor vessel *Christian Sartori* worked her way through northern Lake Michigan bound for Chicago. Waves were running at 25-feet high with occasional ones peaking higher still, with a distance of 50-75 feet between the breaking crests. The wind tore out of the southwest at 60-65 mph and spray from the waves smashing into the bow was clearing the top of her pilothouse. Her captain later remembered the lake was so rough he could only see over the wave tops part of the time. But the rugged little *Sartori* had weathered worse on the wild North Atlantic and she would survive this blow too.

It was about 5:30 p.m. on November 18, 1958 and just about dusk. The typical foul fall weather gave every indication of continuing. It would be a dark and wild night on old Lake Michigan.

The *Sartori's* Captain, Paul Mueller could plainly see the bright lights of the big limestone carrier *Carl D. Bradley* about 4 miles away off the starboard bow. The *Bradley* also gave a sharp, clear return blip on the

135

The German freighter Christain Sartori *witnessed the end of the* Carl D. Bradley. *Stonehouse Collection*

Sartori's radar. To Mueller's eye the *Bradley* was having no discernable difficulty, just running along like an old shoe as the old Lake sailors liked to say. It was a strange American expression. His boat was not having such an easy time of it. On his course of 240 degrees true she bucked heavily into the seas. Unlike the ocean where the distance between wave crests allowed ships to ride up one side and down the other, the crests on the Great Lakes were much closer together, almost like a huge chop. His speed was down to a bare 2 mph! It was going to be a very, very long night.[i]

Suddenly the *Bradley's* lights blinked out. When Mueller looked more intently at where the *Bradley* had been, he was startled to see an explosion of flame and smoke. The circling amber arm of his radar revealed no return of the ship either. She was gone! Mueller immediately altered course and headed for the *Bradley's* last position.

Captain Paul Mueller of the Sartori.
Stonehouse Collection

What Mueller unwittingly witnessed was the cataclysmic breakup and sinking of the self-unloader *Carl D. Bradley* and the death of 33 of her 35-man crew.

Mueller had been a U-Boat skipper during the last war and knew from experience the horror of shipwreck and death on the wild seas. He had seen enough of that on the North Atlantic. He knew if there was any chance for the freighter's crew they needed rescue immediately. He would do his best. The code of sea demanded it.

The 10,028 gross ton *Carl D. Bradley* was built in 1927 at Lorain, Ohio by the American Shipbuilding Company for the Bradley Transportation Company (Michigan Limestone Division) of Rogers City, Michigan. At 623-feet long (65-foot beam, 33-foot depth), she was the largest laker for a number of years. When she first came out she was also the flagship of the fleet, an honor she kept until the 666-foot *John G. Munson* was launched in 1952.[ii] The *Bradley* was also the first vessel through the new McArthur Lock at the Soo when it was opened on July 11, 1943. She was only going

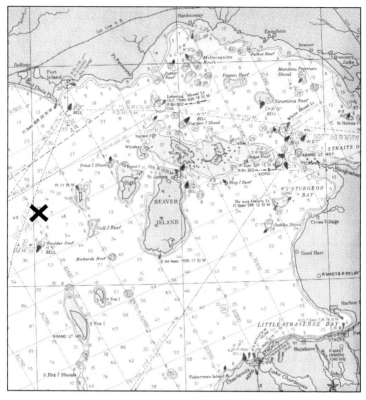

to Algoma Steel with limestone, just above the locks but it was far enough to put her in the history books. Guests on board included a company vice president, the congressman who sponsored the bill authorizing the new lock and the Commandant of the Coast Guard.[iii]

Rogers City is world famous for limestone (calcite), a mineral essential for making steel, chemicals, lime, cement and for construction. The Calcite limestone is heated to 2,300 degrees Fahrenheit and burned to produce lime, which in turn can be used to make soda ash, caustic soda, baking powder, calcium carbide, and other chemicals.

The 623-foot Bradley was the largest laker for a number of years. Stonehouse Collection

Limestone from Calcite also filled the caissons supporting the Mackinac Bridge. The *Bradley* was typical of the self-unloader class of bulk carriers in general use on the Lakes. The traditional arrangement of the pilothouse forward, machinery aft and a large cargo space in between as was (and is) very common.

There were only two watertight bulkheads on the *Bradley*, the collision bulkhead at the bow and one just forward of the engine room. The actual cargo space was subdivided into five separate holds by non-watertight screen bulkheads. The unloading machinery was located in the conveyor room, just forward of the cargo hold. A conveyor tunnel ran through the entire 475-foot length of the cargo hold and conveyor room. The cargo holds were shaped something like a "W" so the stone would naturally migrate to the bottom of the hold where a conveyor belt took it forward to the elevator up to the

The limestone quarry at Rogers City (Calcite) is the largest in the world. Stonehouse Collection

boom conveyor. The tunnel ran the length of the boat using the space in the point of the "W."

The commercial value of the area's calcite deposits was first established in 1908-09. The high quality of the limestone, plus the availability of inexpensive water transportation led to the development of the port of Calcite and the quarry of the same name, both adjacent to Rogers City. It is considered the largest such quarry in the world.[iv]

The port and quarry started operations in 1912 as the Michigan Limestone and Chemical Company and eight years later were purchased by Carl D. Bradley and the U.S. Steel Corporation. After 1923 the fleet ran under the name Bradley Transportation Company. Even after Bradley merged with U.S. Steel in 1952, there was no change in operation. The steamer was named after Carl D. Bradley.

The *Bradley*, with her 160-foot self-unloading boom and conveyor, was designed exclusively for the limestone trade. The new steamer was needed because the company signed a long-term contract with Universal Portland Cement in Buffington, Indiana for stone delivery. In 1929 she carried the largest single cargo ever hauled on the Lakes, anytime, anywhere, 18,114 tons of limestone.[v] She worked continuously in the trade from launching to loss. Her normal schedule kept her operating between the limestone ports on Lake Huron and unloading ports on Lakes Michigan and Erie. She and her fleetmates were a common sight on the Lakes.

The first modern self-unloader constructed for the stone trade was the 303-foot steamer *Wyandotte* built in 1908 by the Great Lakes Engineering Works at Ecorse, Michigan for the Michigan Alkali Company. The firm

The Bradley's *160-foot long boom was an important part of the ships capability.* Stonehouse Collection

regularly hauled stone from Alpena and coal from Pennsylvania to their Wyandotte plant. After due consideration and since a couple of their engineers were former shipbuilders, the company thought it more effective to put the unloading machinery on the ship rather than on land as normally done. The result was a vessel with sloped holds feeding the cargo to a steel pan conveyer running the length of the holds, that in turn dumped product into an elevator leading to a chute and belt conveyor on a swing boom 50-feet long. It may have seemed "Rube Goldbergish" but it worked well and would eventually lead to the self-unloader fleet of today.[vi]

The first vessel on the Lakes with self-unloading ability was the 220-foot wooden steamer *Hennepin*. Built in 1880, she was converted to a self-unloader in 1902 with the addition of a deck-mounted derrick amidships and primitive conveyor boom. The *Hennepin* was lost in a storm off South Haven, Michigan in 1927.[vii]

The first self-unloader (and first vessel) to haul stone for Michigan Limestone and Chemical Company was the

436-foot *Calcite*, built in 1912. As business grew, additional vessels were added. In 1917 the first *Carl D. Bradley* arrived at Calcite Harbor. When the *Carl D. Bradley* (II) was added in 1927, *Carl D. Bradley* (I) was renamed *John G. Munson*. Rogers City was very much a company town and when the new *Bradley* arrived on July 28, it was a holiday celebration. The Calcite plant gave everyone a few hours off to go down to the harbor and watch the new vessel come in. Flags flew everywhere and Mr. Carl D. Bradley was a passenger on his namesake. The next day it was back to business. The new steamer loaded a cargo of stone and headed for Buffington. Like all of the fleet, the *Bradley's* hull was painted gray to help disguise the stone dust that covered her during loading and discharge.

The *Bradley's* captain was 52 year old Roland Bryan from Loundonville, New York, A captain for seven years, he mastered the *Bradley* since 1954 and had 17 years in the company. He started sailing at age 14.

The *Bradley* left Gary, Indiana about 10:00 p.m. November 17, downbound in ballast for Calcite. Before departing both master and mate were advised the forecast called for gale force winds, 50-64 mph from the south with a shift to the southwest anticipated. As she steamed out into the lake winds were already howling at 25-35 mph.

52 year old Roland Bryan was the Bradley's *captain.*
Stonehouse Collection

The threatened gale was strong enough to cause lesser vessels to shelter and wait it out. But ships as large as the *Bradley* were expected to plow their way through. Ships didn't earn their keep by hiding in port every time the Lakes got wavy. Likely no one on board felt any apprehension. It was just another trip. Normal preparations for heavy weather were taken, especially in securing the hatch clamps and boom stays. There was no reason to take any unnecessary risks.

The *Bradley* was running light, without cargo. To stiffen her up, Bryan flooded her ballast tanks outboard and below the cargo holds to keep her steady. Typically she ballasted full aft to get the propeller well into the water, giving her a normal draft of 13-feet, 9 inches forward and 17-feet, 6 inches aft. To achieve this, the forward tanks were only partially full. But again, this was normal procedure.

The *Bradley* passed 11 miles off Milwaukee about 4:00 a.m. on the 18th. Running at 15 mph she reached Sheboygan three hours later. Two other lakers, the *Richard Trimble* and *Governor Miller* were running parallel and slightly shoreward of her.

After passing Milwaukee the wind began to increase, a harbinger of the storm yet to come. As the result of the building seas the *Bradley* increased her water ballast to the maximum extent, roughly two-thirds of the cargo capacity. The extra ballast would help her ride easier. A ship without cargo or adequate ballast, takes a worse beating than one with a normal cargo load. The ballast will help keep the hull lower in the water so it is less vulnerable to the fury of the winds and sledge-hammering of the waves.[viii]

Throughout the day the *Bradley* steamed north, the distance off shore varying from five to 12 miles as the coastline changed. Off Cana Island she came around to a

The Bradley moving through the Soo Locks. Stonehouse Collection

course of 046 degrees true, nearly northeast, cutting across northern Lake Michigan. The new course would bring her to a point between Seul Choix Point and Lansing Shoal where she would turn again to run east to the Straits of Mackinac and Lake Huron. Just before 4:00 p.m. she checked down by 10 rpm to a new speed of 14-15 mph. The slightly slower speed let her ride easier in the now mountainous seas.[ix]

At 4:00 p.m., 42-year-old First Mate Elmer Fleming, came up to the pilothouse and assumed the watch from Captain Bryan. An experienced seaman, Fleming had six years as a first mate and was married with one son. Although a heavy following sea was running, slightly on the steamer's starboard quarter, she was riding comfortably and there was no sign of trouble. The wind had already shifted southwest and increased to the forecast strength of 60-65 mph, known officially as a "whole gale."

Ahead of the steamer, near Boulder Reef, the seas were especially severe. A few hours before the steamer *Johnstown* passed the area and reported very heavy seas. The downbound and loaded steamer *Charles L. Hutchinson* passed earlier in the morning and was forced to throttle back due to the severe seas. When large waves roll into shoal water they will get larger, forced up by the rising bottom.

By this time every other vessel in the northern part of Lake Michigan was heading for shelter. At least eight lakers were anchored or steaming to protection at Green Bay, Garden Island or the Straits of Mackinac.

Shortly after 4:00 p.m. the *Bradley's* radar was turned on and would be used for navigating until her breakup. Why it was not used earlier was never explained. The

radar confirmed the steamer's course was well clear of
Boulder Reef. Bearings at 5:20 p.m. on the north end of
Fox Island and on Gull Island established she was only
slightly to the right of the chart course line.

Between 5:00 and 5:30 p.m., both mate Fleming and a
watchman, Frank Mays, made their way the length of the
ship on the open weather deck from the pilothouse to the
after house. Neither noticed anything unusual. Mays also
went down to the engine room and back to the pilothouse
through the interior tunnel without seeing anything
beyond normal.[x]

The *Bradley* was riding smoothly and taking no seas
over the deck. The motion was so even that sideboards
were not even needed for the mess table! The cook would
set the sideboards to keep plates from sliding on the table
during severe motion. There was no apparent reason to
fear for the vessel.

While aft, Mays pumped water from the sump at the
end of the tunnel, a normal duty of the deck watch. He
noticed there was more water than usual. When he
finished, he returned forward through a watertight door
into the tunnel. Although Mays didn't tighten all the
dogs, he did tighten at least one. Rarely, if ever were
they all secured.[xi]

At 5:20 p.m. the steamer casually radioed her position
to Rogers City, giving an estimated arrival time of 2:00
a.m.[xii] At Captain Bryan's decision the cooks served an
early dinner and the crew was devouring a meal of
hamburgers, French fries, cold tomatoes, sponge cake
and peaches. The captain knew when he turned hard east
to the Straits and Lake Huron the steamer would be
taking the seas on the beam and he wanted the cooks to

The Bradley *was an important part of the fleet.*
Stonehouse Collection

have a chance to clean up and secure before she started
really rolling.[xiii]

Ten minutes later Mate Fleming was startled by a
thud-like noise, followed by an unusual vibration.
Looking aft from the pilothouse he saw the stern sagging!
The damn boat was breaking in two! He immediately
rang the general alarm sounding emergency bells
throughout the ship, while the crew ran for the lifeboats
and rafts. Captain Bryan ran back to the pilothouse and
started blowing the whistle, sending the seven short and
one long blast of the abandon ship signal. Simultaneously
Mate Fleming broadcast a MAYDAY on channel 51.
Fleming would repeat the call until the power to the radio
finally failed. The MAYDAY was immediately answered
by radio station WAD at Port Washington, Wisconsin.

WAD quickly directed all stations to clear the channel for the emergency. WLC in Rogers City also responded to the MAYDAY. Fleming gave the steamer's position as 12 miles southwest of Gull Island. Other shore stations also heard the MAYDAY, including the Coast Guard lifeboat stations at Charlevoix, Michigan and radio station MND at Chesterland, Ohio. Fleming never heard a response from the Coast Guard before the power to the radio failed. Strangely the *Sartori* a bare four miles away did not hear the MAYDAY calls.[xiv]

A shore station that received the call later stated the actual call was, "MAYDAY, MAYDAY, MAYDAY, this is the *Carl D. Bradley*. Our position is approximately 12 miles southwest of Gull Island. We are in serious trouble." Moments later, a voice was heard, "Run, grab your lifejackets. Get the jackets. MAYDAY, the ship is breaking up."[xv]

Mays was in the conveyor room forward when he heard the extraordinary thud, a sound he was unable later to completely describe. He didn't hesitate, running for the ladder topside. Whatever happened, being below wasn't a good idea!

The crew responded quickly to the abandon ship alarm. The men forward put on their lifejackets and ran to the 15 man emergency life raft stored on a cradle just behind the pilothouse. In theory the raft would float off the cradle if the ship sank. There were so many layers of paint on it, some of the crew wondered if it wouldn't just sink! Crewmen aft were observed on the boat deck preparing to lower the starboard lifeboat. The lifeboat was the standard 25-man variety using mechanical davits, manila rope falls and common hooks.

A bare two or three minutes after the strange thud was heard, the *Bradley* heaved upwards at the number 10 hatch and clearly appeared to break in two. Each section was about 300-feet long. When they parted, the rear section with it's lights still blazing swung off to port, while the bow section fell off to starboard. The bow stayed on an even keel and sank from the stern until the weather deck was completely under water when it listed to port, rolled over and plunged to the bottom. It was at this time the life raft floated free.

The stern of the *Bradley* drifted away from the front end on an even keel and then dropped, with the stern rail going down last of all. The starboard lifeboat had been swung forward on it's falls and when the stern section sank, it broke loose and was found floating upside down. Investigators could not determine if any of the crew had time to use it. When the stern section sank, there was a powerful blast of steam and smoke and a bright flash of flame. This was the eruption Captain Mueller saw. It was assumed the red hot boilers exploded when the icy water hit them.

When the *Sartori* finally battled her way to the location where the *Bradley* broke up she searched for survivors until 2:00 a.m. on the 19th, when she was relieved by the Coast Guard buoy tender SUNDEW. About an hour after the sinking the German freighter sighted flares low on the water about a mile off her bow but by the time she reached the area, she found nothing.[xvi]

Numerous Coast Guard stations heard the *Bradley's* MAYDAY call. The Plum Island Lifeboat Station at the tip of Wisconsin's Door Peninsula, dispatched it's motor lifeboat half an hour after the call but due to heavy seas the boat was unable to make any headway and was recalled after fighting the gale for an hour.

The Charlevoix, Michigan Lifeboat Station sent it's 36-foot (CG-36392) motor lifeboat at 6:15 p.m. but again the heavy seas forced its recall. The small lifeboats battling the mountainous waves of a full lake gale presented an exciting spectacle to those people watching from the safety of shore. To the Coast Guardsmen aboard, it was a grim struggle for survival, and a desperate mission to search for men whose lives could be depending on the motor lifeboat's arrival.

The Beaver Island motor lifeboat was not sent because of the gale's severity and a lack of experienced men. Taking a 36-foot motor lifeboat in storm conditions isn't a task for any but highly trained and experienced coxswains and crew. It is no place for men who don't know what they are doing regardless of good intentions.

The 180-foot Coast Guard buoy tender *Sundew* under the command of Lt. Commander Howard D. Muth, was moored at Charlevoix in a 12-hour standby status when the Commander, Group Charlevoix ordered her out. She did a remarkably good job of getting underway and by 6:20 p.m. was heading down the channel, arriving on scene at 10:40 p.m. The term "12-hour status" meant she wasn't expected to get underway in less than that amount of time. *Sundew* only had a skeleton crew aboard, but speed was critical. Waiting for all the crew to join ship wasn't an option, Muth leaving as soon as he had enough crew to do the job. Once *Sundew* arrived on scene she assumed operational control of the search.[xvii] Lt. Commander Muth was at home enjoying a quiet respite

*Lt. Commander Howard Murth skippered
the* Sundew. *Ric Mixter*

when he received a "heads up" telephone call from the Officer in Charge of the Charlevoix Lifeboat Station. He had heard the MAYDAY and figured *Sundew* would be sent so he might as well let the boss know.[xviii]

When *Sundew* cleared the narrow channel from the harbor out into the wild maelstrom of Lake Michigan a large crowd watched her go. Family members, friends of crewmen, townspeople all knew she was sailing to a rescue, but also sailing into danger. It was like the men of the old U.S. Life-Saving Service used to say, "regulations say we have to go out. They don't say anything about coming back." More ominously the 36-foot motor lifeboat from Charlevoix Lifeboat Station trailed along in her wake. It is one thing to face the wild lake in a steel 180-foot ship but to do so in a wood 36-foot lifeboat with an open cockpit is quite another. Once Lt. Commander Muth realized how severe lake conditions were, he ordered the 36-footer back to Charlevoix. The Coast Guard is a relatively new organization, dating from 1915 when the U.S. Revenue Marine Service combined with the U.S. Life-Saving Service to form the present Coast Guard. The Lighthouse Service was added in 1939. From their founding in 1871 the Life-Saving Service wrote a chapter in American maritime history unequalled for courage, tenacity and just plain guts, making rescues in impossible situations! At it's high point, 272 of the lonely little stations dotted American coasts, including 61 on the Great Lakes. Charlevoix Life-Saving Station was established in 1901 and made many thrilling rescues during it's hey day. In 1915 the crew rolled over into the new Coast Guard but the work of saving life during

The Coast Guard 36-foot motor lifeboats were heavily overmatched by the gale. Don Nelson

shipwreck continued with out a miss. It is from the old Life-Savers the Coast Guard draws it's tradition of bravery and rescue.

Aboard *Sundew* the run out to the *Bradley's* last position was horrendous. Muth sealed the ship, not allowing anyone outside of the cabins. It was just too dangerous with waves sweeping hard over her decks. Water sloshed down the stack causing the main electric board in the engineroom to sputter and spark. Since the engines were diesel electric, this was very serious. If the main electric control board shorted out, the engines would stop and *Sundew* goes dead in the water. Because the ship left so quickly, most gear was not stowed properly for sea or lashed down. Virtually every can, box or bottle of food in the galley was destroyed. Propane gas bottles stored on deck for buoy servicing washed away into the oblivion of the wild lake. Every can of paint in the paint locker broke open. When the locker was opened two days later a sea of paint two feet deep poured out! The rolling of the ship was horrible, some crew claiming she reached 55 degrees! The captain later estimated the waves at 25 to 30-feet with some 10 to 15-feet higher! Nearly all the men were seasick. Water getting into the radio room behind the bridge shorted out the main radio and for a while *Sundew* couldn't transmit and reply to the calls from Coast Guard Headquarters in Cleveland. Eight inches of water sloshing across the cabin floor only added to the aura of unreality. Left with the terrible possibility that *Sundew* was gone too, Cleveland was heard to ask other ships if they had seen *Sundew*.

The conditions were so bad the *Sundew's* crew would not go below to sleep. Crew quarters were below the water line and doubtless some felt if she capsized they

The Coast Guard buoy tender Sundew.
Stonehouse Collection

would be trapped. Men in the mess deck tied themselves
to the tables. Moving around on the ship meant holding
fast to something before trying to walk. Everything was
done in slow motion. Between the pounding of the
waves, screaming wind and calliope of slamming,
banging and generally loose objects aboard, the sound
was constant and deafening.[xix]

The 174-foot buoy tender *Hollyhock* was at Sturgeon
Bay, Wisconsin in a two hour status when she was alerted
at 6:15 p.m. Fifteen minutes later she was underway and
on scene at 2:30 a.m. On the northeast run to the wreck,
she reportedly rolled 50 or more degrees like *Sundew*![xx]

The Coast Guard Air Station at Traverse City,
Michigan had one aircraft returning from a southern

Michigan search when notified of the *Bradley* disaster. It was immediately diverted to the *Bradley*, arriving at 7:15 p.m. loitering on the scene throughout the long dark night, dropping a total of 88 aerial flares for surface search illumination. Three Coast Guard HO3S-1 helicopters reached the area at daybreak, the gale delaying their arrival until then.[xxi] These were very marginal machines with a range of 275 miles at 85 miles an hour. The wonder is that they flew at all let alone reaching the scene.[xxii] Additional Coast Guard Albatross seaplanes were deployed as available. They could search but not rescue.

The laker *Robert C. Stanley* was anchored behind Garden Island 20-odd miles to the northeast when she heard the *Bradley's* frantic call. Within an hour this brave ship and crew hauled anchor and was battling through the storm to help a stricken sister. Eventually

U.S. Coast Guard HO35 helicopter. Stonehouse Collection

*U.S. Coast Guard HU16 Albatross seaplane shown
in modern paint scheme.* Stonehouse Collection

nine freighters including the *Transontario*, *Sylvania*,
Algogen, *Sartori*, *Henry Ford II*, *Munson*, *Johnstown* and
Edwin Hoytt II all assisted. Military aircraft from
Selfridge (northeast of Detroit) and Kinross (near Sault
Ste. Marine) Air Force Bases and Glenview Naval Air
Station (north of Chicago) joined in the search effort
when the storm subsided on the morning of the 19th.[xxiii]

Four of the *Bradley* crew, including 46-year-old Elmer
Fleming and 26-year-old deckhand Frank Mays found
themselves in the water when the forward section sunk
beneath them. Luckily they both surfaced near the small
life raft and were able to struggle aboard. When Gary
Strzelecki and Daniel Meredith swam over to the raft,
Fleming and Mays helped them aboard too. There were
other men in the water nearby and although Fleming and
Mays yelled for them to swim to the raft, either they
didn't see the raft or hear the shouts. The men died where
they were, drifting alone in the terrible waves and black
night. The four men held on for dear life as the 8 by 10-
foot wood and metal raft was buffeted by the raging

storm. Even with the sea anchor in the water the raft quickly blew away from the scene.[xxiv]

Mays later recalled watching the stern of the *Bradley* sink. "We could see right into the cargo hold and it was filling with water. Men were running on deck, trying to free the lifeboats. Then she was gone."[xxv]

Numerous times during the long desperate night the life raft overturned in the crashing seas. When it flipped about 10:00 p.m., Meredith could not climb aboard and the others were too weak to bodily haul him on to it. For three hours they held on to Meredith as he dangled from the side. Finally he simply went under and was gone. At the height of the storm the raft's sea anchor rope parted, leaving the small raft at the complete mercy of the waves. Without it they blew farther and faster from the sinking site, the place rescuers would likely first search.

Fleming repeatedly told Mays and Strzelecki not to go to sleep but to stay awake, not to surrender to the overwhelming desire to sleep. Fleming knew if the men did, they would never awaken. Strzelecki suddenly announced he wanted to go swimming. Fleming and Mays tried to keep him aboard but about daybreak he jumped in and just swam away in the 46 degree water. When the first gray streaks of dawn painted the still stormy sky, only Fleming and Mays were left on the raft.[xxvi] Ironically, it wasn't long after Strzelecki left the pair were rescued.[xxvii]

During the long cold night the winds blew the raft to within five and half miles of Gull Island, a considerable distance from the sinking site. Every mile distant from the site decreased the likelihood of being found in time.

At 8:25 a.m. on the 19th, a sharp-eyed lookout on the *Sundew* spotted the raft. Muth deftly maneuvered next to it and his crew dropped a cargo net over the side. A bos'n mate scampered down the slippery net and onto the tossing life raft. With the bos'n providing the muscle, the two survivors were quickly safe aboard the tender.[xxviii] Both were taken to chief's quarters and the ship's corpsman went to work, wrapping them in blankets and carefully warming them up.

Fleming and Mays might have been rescued during the night but the last of their flares failed to ignite. The wet flare just would not fire! The men saw the gloomy bulk of a ship, possibly the *Sartori* slide past perhaps a half mile away but without a flare signal she couldn't see them. Mays remembered, "We could see their spotlights, but it was like looking through a fog or mist. The wind

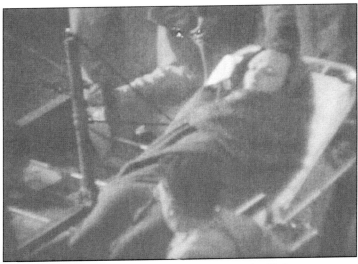

Frank Mays being transported off the
Sundew. *Ric Mixter*

was blowing so hard that water just filled the air. We screamed, but nobody heard."[xxix]

Interviewed later, Fleming remembered, "we climbed aboard the raft and held on with all we had," and "I've never been so cold in my life, ice was beginning to form on my jacket and in my hair." Mays seemed more confident, stating that, "Once on the raft I thought we would be all right. I knew they would find us." A physician later described their survival as, "an amazing feat of human endurance."[xxx]

The man who swam away from the raft Mays and Fleming occupied, was eventually spotted floating in his orange lifejacket by the crew of the freighter *Transontario*. At first the sailors thought he was alive and a panicked call went out for medical help. The Coast Guard responded by packing Beaver Island's 79-year old doctor into a helicopter and heading for the ship. Since the ship was too small to land on, the airmen planned to lower the doctor by a line. However before they arrived at the ship, the message was received the victim was dead, so they returned the doctor to the island.[xxxi]

Later in the morning an overturned lifeboat was sighted four miles east of Gull Island. No one, dead or alive, was seen near it. Several days later the boat was recovered on the shores of High Island, but it gave no evidence of ever being occupied.

Throughout the morning on the 19th, 17 bodies of the crew were recovered in the area north of Gull Island, eight by *Sundew* which used her small boat for the actual recoveries. The men were so heavy with water and their ungainly lifejackets, it took three Coast Guardsmen to haul them over the gunwhale and into the boat. On

Survivors being unloaded from the Sundew. *The lifeboat is in the foreground.* Ric Mixter

Sundew they were carefully laid on the buoy deck and covered with tarps. When *Sundew* arrived back at Charlevoix at 4:23 p.m. on the 19th ambulances and hearses were standing by in the parking lot. Several aircraft chartered by news organizations flew overhead, anxious to shoot film footage of the tragedy. Once *Sundew* moored at the city pier next to the Beaver Island ferry dock, the Charlevoix County medical officer, Dr. Grate, boarded and evaluated Mays and Fleming. Both were immediately sent to the local hospital for treatment. He also officially declared the lifeless bodies dead.[xxxii]

The remains from *Sundew* were taken to a temporary morgue at the Charlevoix City Hall. Later in the day the *Hollyhock* arrived in Charlevoix and added another nine victims to the morgue. *Hollyhock* found the conditions on the lake as bad as *Sundew* experienced. The Chief of the

Boat, James Cropper related, "It was the roughest sea I ever saw and I've seen a few. At times, the pitching and the rolling and the valleys were so deep it looked like all the water had disappeared and was going uphill in front of us. The ocean sailors kid us lake men about our little ponds. I'd better never hear that again. Last night was a visit to Hell."[xxxiii]

That both *Hollyhock* and *Sundew* survived the wild conditions on Lake Michigan is a tribute not only to the skill of their captains and pilothouse watch, but to the builders and designers. Both were originally designed by the old Lighthouse Service and were not intended to fill the heavy rescue role the Coast Guard occasionally asked them to carry out.

An examination at the hospital showed both Mays and Fleming were in relatively good condition and they were given beds in the same room. Although their faces were swollen from exposure there was no frostbite. Both were put to bed surrounded by hot water bottles. Each was also given a stiff shot of whiskey, medicinal of course! After a few minutes their wives joined them, brought by the company to Charlevoix from Rogers City. Later in the evening the men were taken in wheelchairs to a large room for a press conference where they related their experiences.[xxxiv]

As the bodies were identified, company officials performed the terrible job of notifying families of their loss. Everyone with a loved one on the *Bradley* waited for the dreaded knock on the door.

Sundew returned to the search area on the 20th and 21st. The weather was far less severe but the lake was still rough and cold.

———————

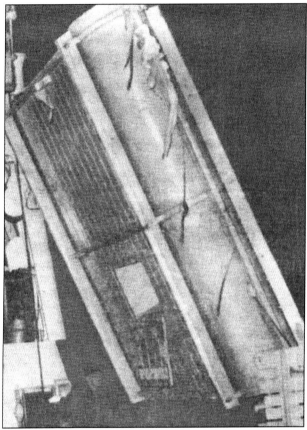

The raft from the Bradley *being unloaded in Charlevoix. It has since disappeared.* Ric Mixter

Sundew unloaded the life raft at the dock along with a lifeboat. The raft apparently later disappeared from Charlevoix and the lifeboat ended up in Put-In-Bay in Ohio. It was eventually taken to the small maritime museum on Beaver Island where it is displayed in a place of honor.[xxxv]

The Coast Guard investigation determined all the victims had drowned. None of the men on watch in the engine room were ever recovered, evidently trapped below when she broke. It is assumed they are still there.

Port Washington radio station WAD assumed radio control during the SAR emergency on channel 51.[xxxvi] This was normal procedure whenever a MAYDAY situation occurred. As soon as the original distress call was heard, WAD broadcast orders for radio silence, repeating it several times as did other stations. The order was lifted the following evening. During the search there was serious interference on the channel caused primarily by unauthorized use of it by vessels on the Ohio and Mississippi Rivers. Additional interference was also caused by the failure of some Great Lakes vessels and stations to maintain the ordered silence. Fortunately the interference did not seriously impair search vessel and aircraft communication.[xxxvii]

With nothing more to be found, the Coast Guard suspended the active search on November 21. Coast Guard aircraft logged a total of 122 hours from November 18 to December 9 without significant result. Although no major portions of the hull of the *Bradley* were found, numerous small pieces of debris were discovered both floating in the area and washed ashore on the desolate beaches of Beaver Island group. Coast Guard helicopters ferried search teams out to comb the lonely beaches of Squaw, Garden, Trout and Whisky Islands. Landing parties from *Sundew* and *Hollyhock* also assisted. There was precious little found. Gull Island yielded a lifejacket and some debris while High provided several lifejackets and the overturned lifeboat spotted by the *Sundew* earlier.

On the 20th a Coast Guard aircraft sighted an oil slick bubbling to the surface about five and one-half miles northwest of Boulder Reef Buoy. When the *Sundew* sounded the area on December 2, she found an unidentified 25-foot pinnacle in 300-feet of water. An immediate resounding by the icebreaker *Mackinaw* failed to find the elusive anomaly. Later attempts by both vessels in February also failed to find it.

Careful soundings were made of the Boulder Reef area since it was considered possible the *Bradley* may have struck it causing the rapid breakup. A thorough check by the Coast Guard failed to find any evidence of grounding and the survey verified the Boulder Reef Buoy was in the proper position.[xxxviii]

Potentially the Boulder Reef was very dangerous. Shoal water of 60-feet or less covered a region about six miles by three miles in area. Although the southwest edge of the shoal is marked by Boulder Reef Buoy, it is easy for an unwary or storm tossed vessel to blunder into the area with deadly consequence.[xxxix]

The Coast Guard investigation, saddled with the job of solving the *Bradley's* loss, did their best. Rear Admiral Joseph Kerrins, Commander, Ninth Coast Guard District (the Great Lakes), arrived with his staff in Rogers City three days after the disaster to begin the inquiry. From there he and his team went to Charlevoix and conducted bedside interviews with Mays and Fleming. This ended the formal investigation although information was collected and considered for another month or so. Delving deep into the facts and circumstance surrounding the casualty, the investigation revealed numerous items and facts bearing directly on the seemingly inexplicable loss.

During the previous winter lay-up (1957-58), numerous cargo hold repairs were made, including replacement of badly deteriorated and loose rivets with carriage bolts. The Coast Guard hadn't approved these repairs prior to their being made as is normal procedure, but when the inspector examined the repairs in progress, he pronounced them adequate. The repairs were reportedly holding during the 1958 season.

Ominously, the *Bradley* was scheduled to receive extensive cargo hold repairs during the coming winter lay-up. The work was to be accomplished at the Manitowoc, Wisconsin yard of the Manitowoc Shipbuilding Company. The repair list included the reconstruction of the tank tops, renewing the cargo hold side slopes and screen bulkheads and installing a centerline bulkhead. Estimated costs were placed at $800,000. Besides replacing worn out material, the work would have increased the longitudinal strength of the steamer.[xl]

Reportedly, the Coast Guard inspectors found about 1,000 rivets on ballast tanks inside the cargo holds missing or eroded. The inspectors wanted them replaced but the owners objected as they were planning to have the tanks replaced the following year anyway. Since the steamer had over 100,000 rivets in the hull, the Coast Guard eventually agreed and investigators felt the rivets in question didn't figure in the sinking.[xli]

In heavy weather a lake will frequently "pop" rivets. The big bulk carriers were built to flex. Their strength isn't in rigidity, but rather in the ability to bend to the force of the waves. Stories are legion about the number of rivets sheared off or popped during the course of a storm. They were literally lost by the bucketful. Crewmen in the mammoth holds would often hear them exploding loose and ricocheting off the steel plates like spent bullets!

The Coast Guard approved planned repairs in February 1958, nearly a year before the work was to be accomplished, as did Lloyd's in October 1957. Following the repairs the *Bradley* was to be drydocked in Chicago for her regular five-year survey. The previous survey was done in Lorain, Ohio in 1953.

The steamer was drydocked in Chicago for a week in May 1958 for repairs after a collision with the steamer *White Rose*. The accident happened at the southeast bend of the St. Clair River, requiring the installation of a 21-foot long bilge plate to replace several damaged smaller plates. During the work a series of hairline fractures were discovered in eight of her bottom plates. The fractured portions of the plates were cut out and replaced with new sections, which were then welded and riveted into place.

At least twice between her drydocking for repairs in Chicago and her November 1958 loss, the *Bradley* suffered bottom damage. The Coast Guard felt there could have been other instances. The first was in the spring of 1958 when she, "rubbed bottom" while departing Cedarville, Michigan at the lower end of the St. Marys River. Cedarville is a major limestone port. Damage was sustained forward, just aft of the collision bulkhead, near the number one water bottom port side. Repairs were not made as the damage was thought to be only minor. In early November 1958 she again rubbed bottom at Cedarville resulting in a 14-inch long fracture in the area of the number seven water bottom, port side, in two strakes. The company's repair force welded a channel bar over the break when the steamer reached Calcite.

Neither the Cedarville damage or channel bar repair was reported to the Coast Guard or to Lloyd's. The incidents only came to light during the loss investigation. Normally such damage warranted an automatic report to the Coast Guard. Why the reports were not made was never explained.

A Coast Guard safety inspection was conducted aboard on October 30. As part of it, a boat drill was held and both lifeboats swung out, launched and 28 crewmen exercised. The inspector was satisfied with the drill. During the inspection the captain stated the repairs to the side tanks done during the 1957-58 lay-up appeared to be holding up well.[xlii]

Reportedly though Captain Bryan complained to friends in letters that the *Bradley* was in bad need of her refit and that she wasn't in any condition to face heavy weather.[xliii]

The last season for the *Bradley* began on April 22 and she completed 43 trips totaling about 27,000 miles before her final run into history. The total trip count for the season was lower than normal since the *Bradley* wasn't operating from July 1 to October 1 due to a lack of trade. Instead she was moored at her Calcite dock with only the lonely steps of a watchman resounding on her steel decks.

The 1958 season was the poorest one for lake freight since 1939, a 19-year low. The demand for iron ore, coal and limestone was short and many ships never even fitted out. By the fall only 180 of 250 vessels operated at all.[xliv]

Chief engineer Buehler worked on the *Bradley* as her chief since 1952 and sailed aboard for nearly her entire history. He knew his boat very well. The actual manager of the fleet was Mr. Normal Hoeft. In 1958 he was only two years into his job and although he had no sailing experience, he had over 33 years with the Michigan Limestone Division. Previous to assuming the manager's position, he worked in the traffic department.

In practice, the masters of fleet vessels were held responsible for the loading and ballasting of their boats. On the *Bradley*, certain methods and sequences were developed which were passed on from master to master and mate to mate. There were no standardized procedures recommended by the company.

The Safety Director of the fleet never received any complaints of hazardous operating conditions on the ship for the four years preceding her loss. However, the safety program was almost completely devoted to industrial type situations and did not include the material or structural conditions of the vessels. The safety program none-the-less was successful as the National Safety Council presented their highest recognition, the Award of Honor to the Bradley Transportation Fleet for the world's record of achieving 2,228,755 injury-free man hours (1,330 days) (April 24, 1955–December 31, 1957).

Following the *Bradley* loss other Bradley crews had second thoughts about the safety of their boats. Reportedly the crew of the *Irvin L. Clymer* sent a petition to the company complaining about her condition. The Coast Guard inspected her with the result she was sent to shipyard for repair. The Bradley Fleet never publicly connected the *Bradley*, petition, inspection and repair.[xlv]

During the course of the investigation the Board made numerous observations based on evidence presented.

Later these observations were used to assist in determining the reasons and circumstances of loss.

The Board observed the ship's trade as extremely hard on vessels. The self-unloaders load and discharge far more cargoes than a conventional bulk carrier. They were also frequently operating in smaller ports, often with shallower channels, thus, "rubbed bottom" fairly frequently. Since the ships tended to run at a higher speed in shallow rivers, bottom damage could be increased.

Looking at the mechanics of the loss, the Board concluded after the initial "thud" the ship traveled not more than a mile before breaking in two and that there is no reason to believe she veered significantly off course during this period.

Why she broke is more difficult to answer, but the investigators felt it was due to excessive hogging stress as the result of her placement in a ballasted condition in the waves encountered at the point of breakup.[xlvi] "Hogging" is a term applied to ships when the bow and stern are drooping. It is the opposite of "sagging" where the midship section has fallen. Yet the Board admitted there was no evidence of any defects in the area of the break. However, there were those hairline fractures in the bottom plates that could have been significant. Still, the Board could fine no relationship between the cracks and the catastrophic breakup.

Undoubtedly the eruption of flames and smoke the *Sartori* saw was caused by water rushing into the hot boilers as the stern sank. Since none of the recovered bodies had any indication of burns or blast, the Board concluded the majority of the explosion was directed out through the stack.

———————

The *Bradley* passed her last annual inspection given at Calcite on April 27, 1958. There was no apparent reason to infer from the testimony or evidence that she wasn't seaworthy when she left Gary on her last trip.

The Board was highly praiseworthy of the efforts of the *Sartori* during her search for survivors. They felt her efforts were in keeping with the very, "finest traditions of the sea" and the fact that the attempt was unsuccessful did not detract from the valiant efforts of the captain and crew. The voluntary assistance of other vessels and aircraft was also commended.

Ominously the Board did state that had the life raft been equipped with rocket or parachute distress signals the survivors might have been located during the night instead of the next morning. For want of proper signal, worth perhaps just a few dollars, good men died.

In spite of the difficulties experienced, communications during the search and rescue operation were considered adequate. Local stations did maintain radio silence when ordered and the heavy interference on channel 51 didn't impede critical on-scene communications.

Investigators felt the owners of the *Bradley* had clearly given complete responsibility for the safety of their vessel to the master and that he had total freedom to either anchor or postpone his departure for reasons of safety. With this in mind, the Board concluded the master had used poor judgment in crossing northern Lake Michigan in the existing weather conditions. He had simply tried to keep too closely to his schedule and paid too little heed to the dangers of the storm. He failed to be a prudent mariner.[xlvii]

Wrapping up the investigation, the Board concluded no aids to navigation or uncharted areas contributed to the loss, nor did any acts of the Coast Guard or other government agencies. Moreover, there was nothing to indicate that licensed men of the *Bradley* performed any, "incompetent acts, inattention to duty, negligence or willful violation of any law or regulation."

An important part of the Board of Investigation's job is to make recommendations of ways to improve vessel safety to hopefully avoid future casualties and methods of increasing the chances of sailors to survive should a casualty occur. For the *Bradley* there were a total of five recommendations. Summarized they were:

1. All jacket type life preservers should be provided with a crotch strap to hold the jacket down on the body with a collar to support the head out of the water. (The strap prevented unconscious survivors from slipping out of the jacket while the collar helped the head stay clear of the water.)

2. A second life raft should be mandatory for all Great Lakes cargo vessels of 300 gross tons or more and that one raft should be located forward and the other aft.

3. Lifeboats on Great Lakes vessels of over 3,000 gross tons should be fitted with mechanical disengaging apparatus instead of common hook systems. (This greatly expedites launching).

4. As required of ocean and coastwise vessels, lifeboats on Great Lakes vessels should be equipped with two painters. (A painter is a rope

in the bow of the boat used for towing or making fast.)

5. All lifeboats and life rafts on Great Lakes vessels should carry a minimum of at least six red parachute flares.

As with all Coast Guard Marine Investigations, the Commandant of the Coast Guard, Vice Admiral A. C. Richmond, reviewed the report, agreeing with some portions and disagreeing with others. The Commandant agreed the greatest likelihood was the breakup of the *Bradley* due to hogging, but disagreed as to why, feeling there was no evidence the break resulted because of an unusual combination of wave conditions and improper or unusual ballasting. As there was no evidence to indicate the ballasting wasn't completely normal and the waves weren't unique to the vessel's history, the Board's conclusion had to be rejected. The survivor's testimony concerning the smoothness of the *Bradley's* ride in the existing sea conditions affirmed this view.

Taking this reasoning further, the conclusion blaming the master for using poor judgment in crossing the lake under those sea conditions was also disapproved.

Although the Board did not suggest any other reason for the loss (and neither did the record), the Commandant felt there were other factors that could have had some connection to it and therefore should not be omitted purely for a lack of substantive evidence.

The Commandant felt the mysterious hairline fractures in the midships area of the hull found in 1957 strongly suggested structural weakness as a viable possibility. The two unreported groundings suffered in the spring and fall of 1958 could have caused unusual hull stresses. Because such possibilities are very real, it is required by regulation that a notice of Marine Casualty be filed with the Coast Guard for each incident, regardless of damage. In the case of the *Bradley* groundings, such notices were not filed.

The question of the overall condition of the *Bradley's* structure could be raised based on the extensive repairs to the cargo hold side slopes, screen bulkheads and tank tops planned for the 1958-59 winter lay-up. It was obvious there was heavy wear and deterioration.

Such possibilities when viewed with the actual method of foundering, breaking in two under sea conditions she should have weathered, certainly leads to the reasoning that an undetected structural weakness was present. This possibility is especially important when the large number of other vessels of similar age and design are considered.

The Commandant felt strongly the one overriding consideration to emerge from the loss was the need for a strong program of technical evaluation to determine if there are any indications of structural failure in other lakers. Such a program was initiated including a reappraisal of inspection methods and procedures to substantially increase the probability of early detection of structural weakness, especially for older vessels. The Commander of the Ninth Coast Guard District (Great Lakes) was directed to study the problem and adopt any reasonable procedures within the framework of existing regulations and to recommend any further regulation needed.

The Board's recommendation concerning the life jacket straps, lifeboat disengaging apparatus, an additional life raft and flares were deftly referred to the Merchant Marine Council for study.

As a conclusion, the Commandant suggested the loss of the *Carl D. Bradley* and her 33 men indicated a need for vessel owners and operators to: "reexamine their responsibilities to establish and maintain safe operating and maintenance procedures."

The U.S. Steel Corporation and the survivors of the *Bradley* reached an agreement in December 1959 for a settlement of $1,250,000 in damages. U.S. Steel had earlier rejected a proposed settlement of $4,750,000. This was one of the speediest cases of its kind ever conducted. Generally they take from three to five years. Originally the survivors sought $16 million and U.S. Steel offered $660,000.[xlviii]

Sums distributed to individuals ranged from nothing at all to $73,309.19. The largest share went to the widow of the second mate and no payment to a deckhand without any dependents. The sums were allocated by a Cleveland lawyer working as a Commissioner with the job of dividing the settlement as fairly as possible among the victims and survivors. For example in the case of the mate the Commissioner determined his life expectancy of 38.2 years times his average wage of $9,980.00. The two survivors received $6,239 and $13,726, with Mays getting the larger and Fleming the smaller. Both reported psychological and physical effects from the disaster.[xlix]

To be absolutely certain that the *Bradley* had not inadvertently struck an uncharted pinnacle or rock, the Army Corps of Engineers tug *Williams* swept the entire area. There was nothing there. Whatever happened, the steamer did not strike an uncharted rock.

The hull of the *Bradley* was finally positively located in 360-feet of water, about 11.5 miles southwest of Gull Island after a search by the Motor Vessel *Submarex* owned by Global Marine Exploration in Los Angles. The 175-foot *Submarex* was brought in from the west coast specifically to perform the *Bradley* survey. Underwater television cameras were the key to confirming the wreck. After a ten-day examination, several important points were made. The camera confirmed earlier sonar traces showing the *Bradley* in one piece. To the camera's eye, the hull was one continuous piece which was inconsistent with the testimony of Mays and Fleming. Although there were fractures in the hull, perhaps from smashing into bottom, the remainder of the hull appeared sound and in fine condition. There was no amplifying information altering the Marine Board finding of fact, conclusions or recommendations, save the observation the steamer did not break in two.[l]

Another tragedy occurred during the survey. The *Submarex* was moored above the wreck and the *Francis*, a local boat from Beaver Island, was hired to make daily supply runs to the vessel. During one of the trips the boat was overcome by the seas and sank with the loss of one life.[li]

What actually happened to the Board recommendations? The recommendation concerning mechanical disengaging apparatus for lifeboats were adopted, with some special provisions. Existing common hooks installations were allowed to continue in use for vessels contracted for prior to May 26, 1965. New installations or replacements would have to be of the mechanical variety.

After study, the Commandant did not concur with the recommendation that all lifejackets be fitted with a collar to support the neck or crotch straps to hold the jackets down on the body claiming the changes only made the jackets too complicated.

The regulation was changed to require two inflatable life rafts on every Great Lakes vessel over 300 gross tons, when crew quarters and work areas were widely separated. The capacity and location were left up to the officer in charge, Marine Inspection.[lii]

The recommendation concerning two painters on Great Lakes lifeboats was approved as was the recommendation to require six parachute flares on each lifeboat and life raft.[liii]

By and large though, the recommendations were accepted, although perhaps not in the most timely fashion. But recommendations are made to prevent future losses for the same cause. The loss of the *Carl D. Bradley* should have served to preclude similar disasters. Considering the loss of the *Daniel Morrell* in 1966 and *Edmund Fitzgerald* in 1975 under circumstances and with results eerily similar to the *Bradley*, such recommendations were clearly insufficient.

Regardless of the Coast Guard conclusion, old-timers had their own beliefs. Captain Forrest R. Pearse, who mastered the *Bradley* for 16 years, thought metal fatigue combined with the effects of a "tidal wave" doomed the ship. Captain Pearse stated, "On the Great Lakes there are certain small areas during a storm that have a lower barometric pressure than the surrounding area. Because of these differences a few waves often build up to twice the height of other waves. Usually there are two or three

The losses of the Daniel J. Morrell *and* Edmund Fitzgerald *were jarringly similar to the* Bradley.
Stonehouse Collection

such giant waves in succession. We were told that waves out there were 25 or 30-feet high. The tidal waves might have been from 45 to 60-feet high. The ship might have been caught on two of those waves, with the bow and stern high on the waves and the midships just hanging in air. That could have caused the breakup. I've experienced those tidal waves many times in the fall. They are just out there. There's nothing to be done about them. You just have to weather them. The *Bradley* was just not so lucky."[liv]

The captain added many of the men on the Bradley ships were excellent sailors but they didn't really want to be on the water. They did it because the jobs were good and they got home often. "But many of them would rather have had jobs on land" he added.

Another *Bradley* Captain, Christian Swarts, who sailed her during the 1952 and 1953 seasons, remembered Captain Roland Bryan as a, "good sailor and a good man." He said, "Seamen know a thing like this can happen, but they never think it can happen to them. This time it did."[lv]

Perhaps the best testimony came from Captain Roland Bryan who rode her to the bottom. Ten days before she sank he wrote a letter to a woman friend stating in part, "This boat is getting pretty ripe for too much weather. I'll be glad when they fix her up. Supposed to go to Manitowoc this fall to lay-up. They say it won't be until the 10th of December. I hope it's before that. It's been a screwy season all the way through." Bryan was a bachelor and often wrote to a widowed school teacher in Port Huron.[lvi]

Comments made by watchman Frank Mays supported the captain's letter. He stated when loading rust poured from the side of her holds and he saw rust around the edges of the bulkhead separators at the bottom where they joined the cargo holds. Bulkheads were rusted so badly he could see into the next cargo hold. He said the cargo hold, "was not much good" and she was a "rotten ship." There were also holes in the top of the ballast tank tops. When the tanks were filled water would sometimes slosh through the rust holes. Some of the men joked about her being held together by rust! Mays went to work for the company in March 1957 and worked in the ship for three days in the spring of 1958 and again from October until her loss.[lvii]

The personal impact of the loss of the *Bradley* was devastating. Reportedly over 53 children were made fatherless by the sinking and 23 women became widows. The 25 men who made Rogers City their home meant about three percent of the population had relatives on the laker. It was a heavy cross for the small town to bear.[lviii] The wife of the wheelsman, Earl Tulgetske told a reporter, "I always watched the boats and I knew the town lived by them. Now the town is dying by them."[lix]

When the victims were taken home to Rogers City they were placed in state in the gymnasium of Rogers City High School. Hundreds of relatives and friends marched past the caskets paying their silent respect. A community memorial service followed. A six-foot high white flower anchor inscribed "Farewell Shipmates," stood center stage with fifteen caskets standing by, arranged about the floor. After a day the remains were moved to churches or funeral homes for additional

St. Ignaious Church was the scene of many of the
Bradley *funerals.* Stonehouse Collection

Many of the victims were "laid out" in the Rogers
City High School gym. Ric Mixter

services. Ten were taken to the St. Ignaious Catholic School gymnasium for a Roman Catholic service. The crews of the four Bradley Fleet boats in town, *Calcite*, *White*, *Clymer* and *Munson,* were given leave to attend services. The four other ships which were at sea; *Robinson*, *Cedarville*, *Rogers City* and *Taylor* were instructed to conduct a shipboard memorial service as close to noon as conditions permitted. The Michigan Limestone plant also closed for the funerals.[lx]

Following the services the entire town of nearly 4,000 formed into the funeral procession. Thirteen of the victims were buried in the Rogers City cemetery. A 30-day period of official mourning followed.[lxi]

A special trust fund was started for the fatherless children. By July 24, 1959 it had reached nearly $150,000.[lxii] Eventually the trust fund totaled $157,000.[lxiii]

Memories die hard, especially in a small town trying to over come a tragedy as large as the *Bradley*. For a while the widows and children were pointed out to strangers. "That's Mrs. …she lost her husband on the *Bradley*." A year after the loss, two of the 23 widows remarried and seven moved away. Fourteen were still in the area but all were trying to get on with their lives.[lxiv]

The two survivors took different paths after they recovered from the wreck, not that a person ever really recovers from such an ordeal. Mays, "swallowed the anchor," as the old sailors said and took a job ashore. He never sailed the Lakes again. Fleming returned to the boats eventually retiring as captain of the *Cedarville*. He died of a heart attack in 1969.[lxv]

The loss of the *Cedarville*, another Bradley boat, was another hard blow against Rogers City. Ten men were

The memorial encompasses both the Carl D. Bradley *wreck and* Cedarville, *both with a devastating local impact.* Stonehouse Collection

lost with the ship when she sank in Lake Huron just east of the Straits of Mackinac in 1965. Nine of the victims hailed from Rogers City.

A small granite marker down by the waterfront remembers the men lost in both ships. It is little enough tribute to the dead, but certainly far more than most sailors ever received.

The great mystery of the *Bradley* was the conflict between what Mays and Fleming saw, the ship break in two on the surface and the underwater survey by *Submarex*, reporting the ship in one piece. This was a very important distinction as it directly affected the liability of the company. If the *Bradley* was overwhelmed by the gale and sank, it could be called an "Act of God" and the company certainly was not liable for such things. The insurance payout to the victims was therefore comparatively small. However, if the ship broke on the surface, then it could be argued she was not in good structural condition, which of course increased the company's liability and insurance payouts to victims.

When the evidence was examined the conclusion drawn, doubtlessly assisted by the company's admiralty attorneys, was interpreted to mean the sinking was an "Act of God." In effect, the ship was structurally sound but the storm was too powerful for her. The company could not be held liable for such an unfortunate and uncontrollable event!

What Mays and Fleming saw was discounted. Considering the terrible storm, the stress of the sinking, the loss of so many of their friends, it is understandable that they "thought" they saw what they clearly, by the evidence, could not have. Mays and Fleming knew what they saw, regardless of the smooth talking lawyers. But they could not prove it, until Fred Shannon, Mount Morris, Michigan businessman, underwater explorer and documentary film maker took an interest in the wreck.

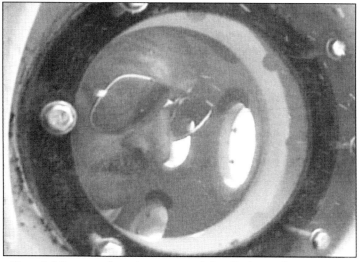

Frank Mays at the view port of the Delta sub. Ric Mixter

Shannon partnered with renown maritime artist Jim Clary who garnered expedition funding and acted as director of the mission. The team used *Delta*, a small two-man submarine operated by California based Delta Oceanographics to explore the *Bradley*. Shannon used the same sub the previous year to document the *Edmund Fitzgerald* in Lake Superior. Rough weather delayed the first dive for four days but on Tuesday, August 15, 1995 the lake calmed enough for an attempt to reach the wreck. 63-year old Mays was aboard with the sub operator for the first dive. As *Delta* descended the crew topside anxiously listened as the operator called out the depths. Visibility was terrible. Finally Mays called out, "There's the name Carl D. Bradley," which was clearly visible on the port aft section of the hull. It was the first views seen of the sunken vessel after nearly forty years. A small plaque engraved with the names of the *Bradley* crew and expedition members was later placed near the engine room, believed to be the resting place for many of the crew.[lxvi]

Bad weather and silt severely limited the diving and Mays was unable to point out the break in the hull. Visibility at depth was little more than five feet and there was deep concern over the exact location of the Bradley's huge unloading boom. The crew had planned 24 dives, but could make only five and of those, only two actually saw the wreck. Clary made the second and longest dive and was able to document much of the stern of the sunken ship. The privately funded exploration reportedly cost $150,000.[lxvii] In spite of the lack of success, the group vowed to return.

Shannon, Clary, and Frank Mays returned to the *Bradley* in May 1997, and was able to thoroughly document the wreck using a deep ocean, remotely operated video camera.

This time they found the "smoking gun," discovering the ship broken in two at the bottom of a trench. Both sections are upright, about 90-feet apart and almost in line. From the video evidence the aft port corner of the forward section was apparently the first part to hit bottom. A large stress fracture was discovered on the port side and the forward mast, main mast, radar and steering pole appear to have separated from the steamer. All pilothouse window glass is gone. Incredibly, the 160' unloading boom is still secure and lashed in place.

The aft section rests at a 20-degree angle with the stern off the bottom. Many hatch covers and rail stanchions are missing or damaged. Coal is scattered around the wreck.[lxviii]

Working from the resulting videotape, Clary produced a series of remarkable and riveting illustrations depicting the *Bradley* on the bottom.[lxix]

It took 39 years to prove it, but Fleming and Mays were right all along! The *Bradley* did break on the surface!

Today with the advent of "mixed gas," often called "technical" diving, the *Bradley* is becoming an increasing target for underwater exploration. Previously sport divers were restricted to roughly a 150-foot depth but with the new technology, 360-plus depths are common. Even the *Edmund Fitzgerald* at 550-feet has been reached by technical divers. The first diver on the *Bradley* was Mirek Standowicz from the boat of Pat and Jim Stayer of Out of the Blue Productions. He reportedly spent a dozen minutes on the bow videotaping. Doubtlessly as the *Bradley* is given closer scrutiny by divers, more of her secrets will be revealed.[lxx]

Both the *Hollyhock* and *Sundew* have since been decommissioned by the Coast Guard. *Hollyhock* was decommissioned in March 1982 and sold commercial. Renamed *Good News Mission Ship* she was eventually sunk as an artificial reef off Pompano Beach, Florida in 1990.[lxxi] Her name continues in a new 225-foot seagoing buoy tender built by Marinette Marine Corporation in Marinette, Wisconsin and commissioned in 2002. *Sundew* was decommissioned in 2004 and is presently a museum ship in Duluth.

Footnotes

[i]Marine Board of Investigation: Foundering of the *SS Carl D. Bradley*, July 7, 1959.

ⁱⁱMarine Board of Investigation.

ⁱⁱⁱhttp://vos.noaa.gov/MWL/dec_04/bradley.shtml.

ⁱᵛGerald F. Micketti, *The Bradley Boats*, (Traverse City: Gerald F. Micketti, 1995), p. 4. Rogers City and Calcite are often used synonymously.

ᵛWilliam Ratigan. *Great Lakes Shipwrecks and Survivors*, (Grand Rapids: Wm. B. Eerdmans Publishing Company, 1977).

ᵛⁱMacketti, *Bradley*, pp. 4-5.

ᵛⁱⁱMacketti, *Bradley*, p. 5.

ᵛⁱⁱⁱMarine Board of Investigation.

ⁱˣMarine Board of Investigation.

ˣMarine Board of Investigation.

ˣⁱ"Dogs" are small bent metal fittings used to close the doors to watertight compartments, hatch covers, etc.

ˣⁱⁱMarine Board of Investigation.

ˣⁱⁱⁱ*The Gazette*, September 2, 1994.

ˣⁱᵛStatement of Elmer H. Fleming, First Mate of the Steamer *Carl Bradley*, U.S. Coast Guard Investigation.

ˣᵛ*Daily Mining Journal*, November 19, 1958.

ˣᵛⁱMarine Board of Investigation.

ˣᵛⁱⁱMarine Board of Investigation; http://www.duluthport.com/mag2004/fall04/storm.html.

ˣᵛⁱⁱⁱhttp://www.jacksjoint.com/bradleydisaster.com; http://www.shipwreckmuseum.com/stories.phtml?artid+30.

ˣⁱˣStonehouse Collection, *Carl D. Bradley*.

ˣˣMarine Board of Investigation; Francis E. Martin, "Breakdown on Boulder Reef: the Tragedy of the *Bradley*," (*Journal of Beaver Island History*, Volume 5, 2002), p. 142.

ˣˣⁱMarine Board of Investigation.

ˣˣⁱⁱhttp://www.uscg.mil/hq/g%2Dcp/history/ac%5Fsikorsky%5Fho3s.html.

ˣˣⁱⁱⁱ*Search and Rescue Operation for* SS Carl D. Bradley, Public Information Office, Ninth Coast Guard District, n.d.; Marine Board of Investigation.

ˣˣⁱᵛA "sea anchor" is a drag, usually made with a hawser

attached to a large funnel shaped canvas bag. A sea anchor will serve to keep a life raft steady in the waves as well as help maintain relative position. When the sea anchor was lost the winds were able to blow the raft far from the area the Coast Guard was searching.

[xxv]*Detroit News*, November 13, 1988.

[xxvi]*Detroit Times*, November 11, 1958; Fleming Statement.

[xxvii]*Detroit News*, November 13, 1888.

[xxviii]Different sources give times varying from 08:15 a.m. to 8:25 a.m.

[xxix]*Detroit News*, November 13, 1988.

[xxx]*Daily Mining Journal*, November 20, 1958.

[xxxi]Francis E. Martin, "Breakdown on Boulder Reef: the Tragedy of the *Bradley*," (*Journal of Beaver Island History*, Volume 5, 2002), p. 144.

[xxxii]http://www.jacksjoint.com/bradley_disaster.htm.

[xxxiii]*Detroit Times*, November 20, 1958.

[xxxiv]Stonehouse Collection, *Carl D. Bradley*.

[xxxv]http://www.jacksjoint.com/bradley_disaster.htm.

[xxxvi]Search and Rescue.

[xxxvii]The use of VHF/FM communication is characterized by long-range signal propagation and thus interference. The current VHF/FM system virtually eliminates the interference problem.

[xxxviii]Marine Board of Investigation.

[xxxix]A lighted bell buoy.

[xl]Marine Board of Investigation.

[xli]*Daily Mining Journal*, December 1, 1958.

[xlii]Marine Board of Investigation.

[xliii]Ratigan, *Great Lakes*.

[xliv]*Daily Mining Journal*, December 8, 1958.

[xlv]Pat and Jim Stayer, Tim Juhl, as told to, *If We Make It Til Daylight, the Story of Frank Mays,* (Lexington, Michigan: Out of the Blue Productions, 2003), pp. 128-129.

[xlvi]Marine Board of Investigation.

[xlvii]Marine Board of Investigation.

xlviii*Milwaukee Journal*, December 5, 1959.

xlix*Detroit Free Press*, n.d.

l Marine Board of Investigation.

li Francis E. Martin, "Breakdown on Boulder Reef: the Tragedy of the *Bradley*," (*Journal of Beaver Island History*, Volume 5, 2002), p. 146.

lii This is rather interesting as the *Daniel J. Morrell*, lost in 1966 did not carry inflatable life rafts, but rather the old style.

liii*Hearings Before the Subcommittee on Merchant Marine and Fisheries*, House of Representatives, Ninety-Fourth Congress, July 26, 1976.

liv*Detroit Free Press*, November 21, 1958.

lv*Detroit Free Press*, November 21, 1958.

lvi*Detroit Free Press*, November 22, 1958.

lvii*Detroit Times*, November 22, 1958.

lviii*Daily Mining Journal*, November 21, 1958; *Detroit News*, November 13, 1988.

lix*Detroit Free Press*, November 20, 1958.

lx*Detroit Free Press*, November 22, 1958; the last body was recovered on November 21, by the steamer *Trans-Ontario*.

lxi*Detroit Free Press*, November 23, 1958.

lxii*Detroit Free Press*, July 24, 1959.

lxiii*Detroit News*, November 13, 1988.

lxiv*Detroit Free Press*, November 8, 1959.

lxv*Chips*, November 26, 1988.

lxvi*Chips*, August 21, 1995; *Mining Journal*, August 16, 1995; Interview, James Clary, February 14, 2005.

lxvii*Mining Journal*, August 28, 1995.

lxviii*Great Lakes Seaway Log*, May 27, 1997; *World Maritime News*, May 16, 1997; Interview, James Clary, February 16, 2005.

lxix http://www.jclary.com/.

lxx http://www.ship-wrecks.net/shipwreck/Fall2001.isp.

lxxi http://www.uscg.mil/hq/g%2Dcp/history/WEBCUTTERS/Hollyhock_1937.html.

✳ 8

CEDARVILLE

May 7, 1965

The *Cedarville* cleared Calcite (Rogers City, Michigan) at 5:01 a.m. May 7, 1965 bound for Gary, Indiana with a full cargo of 14,411 tons of open hearth limestone. She carried a crew of 35. As she churned her way north on Lake Huron to the Straits of Mackinac the ship was making revolutions for full speed, about 12.3 mph. The whistle was blowing the required Great Lakes fog signal since light fog covered the lake, reducing visibility to about a mile. At approximately 8:42 a.m. when she passed the Cheboygan Traffic bell buoy close aboard, visibility was down to half a mile. She changed course to 302 degrees true for the Mackinac Bridge. Because of the fog the captain gave a security call on both channel 16 (FM) and channel 51 (AM) announcing his new course and position.[i]

Five minutes later the downbound *Benson Ford* contacted the *Cedarville*. As dictated by good procedure, the two vessels established a passing arrangement and sounded a one-blast signal for a port-to-port crossing. In effect the two ship would pass each other on the port side.

The steamer Cedarville carried a cargo of 14,411 tons of stone on her last run. Stonehouse Collection

The *Cedarville* also swung a few degrees to starboard to assure a safe crossing. The two ships passed about a half-mile apart without incident. Neither saw the other in the fog. So far all was normal.

The *Cedarville* continued on it's course of 305 degrees true to stay clear of downbound traffic. Three or four miles from the bridge she made radio contact with the downbound German freighter *Weissenburg* still in the Mackinac Bridge channel, west of the bridge. Since the *Weissenburg* said she was heading down the South Channel, the one the *Cedarville* was running up, the two captains arranged for a safe port to port passing. To be extra safe the *Cedarville* altered course five more degrees to starboard. Visibility was now down to 1,200 feet.[ii]

The lookout on the *Cedarville* stationed on the port bridge wing about 25 feet back from the bow, reported hearing underway signals from the bearing of the Mackinac Bridge. The captain also heard the signals in the pilothouse and later stated he reduced speed to slow ahead in response.

At 9:32 a.m. the *Weissenburg* passed under the bridge. About then she called the *Cedarville* to let her know a Norwegian freighter was running ahead of her. To this point nothing had been heard from the Norwegian. She was quiet as a tomb. The captain of the *Cedarville* called the Norwegian several times to arrange a passing agreement but received no answer. It was every captain's nightmare. A ghost vessel running somewhere ahead in the fog, unresponsive to the radio and in your lane. Who is she? Most important, what is she going to do?

In the *Cedarville* pilothouse the third mate was tracking an unknown vessel on radar, later determined to be the Norwegian freighter *Topdalsfjord*. As the range between the two ships decreased, there are two versions of events.

The *Cedarville's* wheelsman said the course was changed starboard to 325 degrees true and speed reduced to half speed. The mate reported the stranger closing in with a constant bearing. The *Cedarville* sounded a one blast port to port passing signal. Shortly the other ship magically appeared out of the fog about 100 feet distant! The *Cedarville's* captain immediately ordered full ahead and hard left in a frantic effort to swing clear and avoid a collision. The wheelsman, Leonard Gabrysiak, usually worked as a third mate. Before leaving Calcite a more senior man joined the ship so Gabrysiak bumped down to wheelsman. Without question, Gabrysiak was well qualified to comprehend events and the situation.[iii]

The captain however had a different recollection, claiming he was proceeding slow ahead on 310 degrees true when the mate reported the other ship was "widening out to port." He claimed he blew a one blast port to port signal and attempted several times again to contact the stranger on radio without success. His radio calls went unanswered. On the mate's radar recommendation he turned more to starboard to provide a greater margin of safety. When the *Topdalsfjord* appeared out of the fog 900 feet away he ordered hard right and full ahead and as the *Cedarville's* bow passed ahead of the *Topdalsfjord's* bow he ordered hard left to try to swing the stern clear.

Regardless of the differing versions, the Norwegian's bow slammed into the *Cedarville* at the number seven hatch port side flooding the number two cargo hold and number four ballast tanks. It was a fatal wound.

The *Topdalsfjord* left Milwaukee at 6:30 p.m. on May 6 bound for Fort William, Ontario on Lake Superior with 1,800 tons of general cargo. Her voyage originated in Denmark.

The Norwegian American Lines freighter *Topdalsfjord* was built in Goteburg, Sweden in 1959. Home ported in Oslo, Norway, the 423-foot, 5,839 gross registered ton ship was powered by a powerful 6,200 horsepower

The Norwegian freighter Topdalsfjord *was a frequent visitor to the Great Lakes.* Stonehouse Collection

diesel. Her master, Rasmus Haaland was a licensed officer for 29 years and had made 19 trips to the Great Lakes. Her sharply raked bow was reinforced for working in ice. Doubtless the reinforcement helped her in the collision.

The freighter came north up Grays Reef Passage running at full speed, 17.4 mph. When she cleared White Shoal she turned east for the bridge on a course of 95 degrees true. About 9:03 a.m. she reduced speed due to the fog and picked up an unidentified vessel on radar running westbound near the bridge. *Topdalsfjord* kept the *Weissenburg* informed of the change in speed and unknown vessel since she was running close behind. The unknown westbound vessel and the eastbound Norwegian freighter passed safely, seen only on the radar screen. Due to the heavy fog near the bridge, the *Topdalsfjord* added a second bow lookout .

Because of the heavy fog the *Topdalsfjord* decided to take the South Channel rather than the shorter but tighter Round Island Passage. It was a fateful decision. Round Island Passage, running between Mackinac Island and Round Island, was the normal route for Lake Superior bound vessels. The radio operator supposedly made several radio calls announcing the new course on channels 16 and 51 without reply. There is no evidence the calls were ever heard by anyone. Soon after the calls were made a radar target was picked up 20 degrees relative to the starboard bow and about a mile and a half distant. Soon fog signals were heard from the same area. The fog signal of another vessel, which later was determined to be the steamer *J. E. Upson*, was heard 60 degrees relative, off the starboard bow. Earlier in the day, well before dawn,

The J.E. Upson anchored nearby after striking Grays Reef Light in the fog. Stonehouse Collection

Blinded by the fog, the steamer Upson *smashed into lonely Grays Reef lighthouse.*

the *Upson* smashed bow on into Grays Reef Lighthouse, 20 miles or so west of the bridge. Regardless of the fog, how the big steamer managed to hit the lighthouse is remarkable. The three Coast Guardsmen manning the light must have had the shock of their lives! Luckily no one was injured and flooding on the *Upson* was minor. After reporting the collision to the Coast Guard the steamer was ordered to anchor east of the bridge. It was the anchored *Upson* signals the Norwegian crewmen heard.

The *Weissenburg's* signal was still audible astern. Due to the confusing situation the *Topdalsfjord* maintained a course of 108 degrees true and slowed to dead slow ahead, about 3-4 knots. As the range decreased with the approaching ship, the bearing changed to 29 degrees relative to the starboard bow. At a range of half a mile the Norwegian increased speed to half ahead, about 6.5 knots. The radar target became so large and confusing, an accurate bearing couldn't be taken. Puzzled, the *Topdalsfjord* rang stop engines at 9:43 a.m. Even with engines stopped, her momentum carried her forward. Visibility was about 600 feet.[iv]

As the *Topdalsfjord* was engulfed in the fog her captain standing outside on the starboard bridge wing heard a very long blast close on his starboard bow. Within seconds the *Cedarville* was sighted approximately 250 feet from the bow. He immediately rang for full astern on the engine telegraph and placed the helm hard right. The result was the Norwegian running nearly perpendicular to the *Cedarville*. At 9:45 a.m. the reinforced ice bow cut

The Topdalsfjord's *bow was pushed back in the collision.* Stonehouse Collection

deep in the *Cedarville* at nearly a right angle. The impact was only moderately felt and the bow remained in the stone carrier just briefly as the forward motion of the *Cedarville* continued, pulling the ships apart and the laker disappeared in the fog. A minute later the Norwegian drifted to a stop. Since the time between sighting each other was so short, neither vessel blew a danger signal. The exact point of collision was 78 degrees true, 6,600 feet from the south tower of the bridge.

When she hit the *Cedarville* a full complement was on duty in her pilothouse, including captain, chief officer, second officer, radio officer and wheelsman. A lookout stood duty at the bow, 200 feet ahead. As with the *Cedarville* all navigational equipment was in good working order. There was no mechanical failure.

Immediately following the collision the *Topdalsfjord* drifted in the pea soup fog and readied her two lifeboats in case they were needed to rescue survivors from the other vessel. When it was learned the *Cedarville* sank, the boats went looking for survivors. At 11:15 a.m. the *Topdalsfjord* proceeded to an anchor near Mackinaw City at the south end of the bridge, as directed by the Coast Guard. Her boats returned to her at about 4:00 p.m. without locating anyone from the *Cedarville*.

The Norwegian freighter suffered extensive damage to 11 feet of her bow. However her collision bulkhead was not damaged so flooding was confined to the forepeak. She eventually continued on to Port Arthur, Ontario on Lake Superior for repairs estimated at $30,000. No one on the *Topdalsfjord* was injured.

By contrast the *Cedarville* was fatally damaged. She was holed at the number 7 hatch port side with damage extending above and below the waterline. Her number 4 port side tank and double bottom was also injured and water was pouring into the number 2 cargo hold. She developed an immediate list to port. The design of the *Cedarville* was such that if a cargo hold flooded she would sink since the tunnel containing the unloading conveyor ran the length of the ship and was not watertight. If water enters one cargo hold, it will flood into all holds via the tunnel. There was no stopping it.[v]

As soon as possible following the collision the *Cedarville* immediately stopped her engine, rang the general alarm, broadcast a MAYDAY call and dropped the port anchor. A separate call was made to the small Coast Guard station on Mackinac Island alerting them of the accident. The captain then called the *Weissenburg* asking for the name of the Norwegian freighter. In the confusion of the impact he didn't see it. The captain also notified the Bradley fleet of the accident.

The chief mate rushed back to assess damage and soon reported to the captain that a tremendous amount of water was flooding into number 2 hold. He said he tried to rig the collision tarp over the impact hole, but the jagged edged gap was too big for it to work. No ship carried a tarp big enough to cover such a massive hole.

The *Cedarville's* lifeboats, on the aft deckhouse, were swung out and lowered to the spar deck level. All the crew except the men on watch or working in the engine room, mustered by the boats and stood by. The *Cedarville* also had two life rafts; a 15 man raft forward and a 25 man raft aft; both stored to float free if the ship sank. Crewmen recalled there was no panic, confusion or delay. Everything went like a drill. Immediately following the collision the wheelsman ran below for lifejackets since none where kept in the pilothouse. On returning, he immediately donned his. The captain and mate didn't, leaving theirs on the floor.

The chief engineer F. Lamp and his first assistant W. Tulgetske, went to the engine room to get ready to start the pumps although as yet there was no order from the bridge to do so. Tulgetske ran up to the deck and checked the damage then returned to the engine room. Based on his observations and on their own decision, the men started pumping number 4 port side and bottom tanks. Four minutes later the bridge called down and ordered them to counter flood the starboard side in an effort to bring the ship level. Soon all pumps were banging away, either working to counter flood or empty the number 4 tank and bottom tanks. At this point some of the men left the engine room rather than be trapped below decks. Shortly after they reached deck, the ship capsized.[vi]

Once the captain and mate evaluated the damages, the *Cedarville* tried to raise her anchor to head for shallow water in an effort to beach the vessel but the anchor fouled on the bottom. It took a few minutes of "hard astern" to pull it free. After it finally came loose the captain headed her for the beach. If she could slide up on a nice sandy bottom salvage would be comparatively easy. He ordered hard left and revolutions for full speed on a heading of 140 degrees true, roughly southeast. The course was the one recommended by the third mate, still at the radar. The damaged *J.E. Upson* was anchored in the fog somewhere off Old Point Mackinac and it was important to clear her as the *Cedarville* ran for the beach. One collision was enough![vii]

———————————

The unloading boom allowed the Cedarville *to discharge cargo at many locations with ease.*
Stonehouse Collection

As the *Cedarville* slowly gathered way, the captain called the *Weissenberg* warning her she was moving and asking her to keep clear. Regardless of full power, the *Cedarville* never exceeded 6 mph. She was starting to settle and pushing too much water. Wheelsman Gabrysiak, concerned with being trapped in the pilothouse if she suddenly rolled, asked permission to lock the doors open. The captain agreed.[viii] The captain of the *Weissenberg*, an impartial observer, believed the *Cedarville* was sinking and his help would be needed.

At 10:25 a.m., with the *Cedarville* virtually awash, she suddenly rolled to starboard, and capsized in 102 feet of water. She traveled a mere 2.3 miles from the point of collision and had another two miles to go before reaching her intended beaching point.

When the *Cedarville* started to roll the crew mustered by the lifeboats made a hurried attempt to launch them. The number 1 lifeboat on the high side was never released from the hooks and sank with the ship. The men managed to get the number 2 lifeboat free of the falls and climb in as the ship sank beneath them. Both life rafts floated free as intended. Most of the crew on deck were thrown into the cold water and had to swim for it.

One of the men remembered seeing the third mate still in the pilothouse struggling to get a lifejacket on when the vessel rolled. The captain never did get his on. He was later rescued floating in the lake clinging to it.

Wheelsman Gabrysiak remembers what happened when the *Cedarville* rolled. "I went over with the boat. I must have hit the cables from the boom. I had these big marks all over me. Then I broke free and started going down due to the suction. I'm looking through my eyelids and at first the water is light, then it's getting darker and darker. Pretty soon it's black. It felt like I was near the bottom. My first thought was if I get caught in the

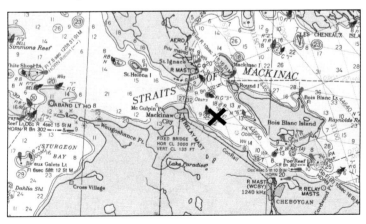

undertow (I'm gone.). I started praying. I started on the Hail Marys. By the time I finished five Hail Marys I started going up. I could see the water getting lighter but I couldn't hold my breath any longer. My lungs were ready to burst. I have to take a breath. When I did I took a lot of water in.....(when I reached the surface) I shot out of the water (he was wearing a lifejacket thus explaining the explosive buoyancy). I could hear voices but they were in the distance. I didn't see anybody. Pretty soon I saw a lifeboat so I gave the old two-finger whistle. I can whistle pretty good so soon they spotted me. They came alongside me, I grabbed the gunwale and passed out. I don't remember anything after that. The next thing I remember was being aboard *Mackinaw*."[ix]

Since the captain of the *Weissenberg* was so convinced she would sink, he followed the *Cedarville* as the wounded ship ran for the beach, tracking her on radar. Both of the German's lifeboats were prepared for immediate launching. If the *Cedarville* sank, the German captain wanted to be fully prepared to give aid. At 10:30 a.m. the bow lookout heard cries for help from men in the water ahead. Three minutes later the lookout sighted the men. Within minutes the *Weissenberg's* boats were launched and quickly hauled six survivors from the frigid 36 degree water. The number 2 lifeboat and aft life raft were also found and towed back to the *Weissenberg* with another 21 survivors. Five of the men were picked up by the freighter when her captain deftly maneuvered the big ship directly alongside the a life raft. One survivor described it as an incredible feat of seamanship. He was sure the freighter would run them down! Aboard ship the victims were bundled in blankets and given stimulants.[x] One of the crew was recovered dead from drowning and another died an hour after coming aboard from shock and exposure.[xi]

On receipt of the MAYDAY call the Coast Guard station at Mackinac Island dispatched a 40-foot utility boat at 9:55 a.m. and a 36-foot motor lifeboat soon after. The 40 boat arrived on scene 35 minutes later but found no survivors. All the men still living were rescued by the *Weissenberg*. The Coast Guard did find the empty forward end life raft.

Coast Guard icebreaker *Mackinaw* quickly got underway from her Cheboygan, Michigan homeport at 10:42 a.m. She was 18 miles distant and arrived at 12:04 a.m. when she assumed control of the search and rescue operation. At 12:48 a.m. the *Mackinaw* moored up to the *Weissenberg* and transferred the survivors. Eventually they were taken to Mackinaw City. Given the opportunity for "stimulants" aboard the *Weissenberg* and the notoriously dry Coast Guard, it was likely a transfer the men perhaps didn't exactly appreciate.

The Coast Guard conducted search operations until May 12, including aircraft from Traverse City, the tug *Naugatuck* and buoy tender *Sundew*. Nothing more was found.

Salvage divers reported the *Cedarville* lying deck down with the starboard rail broken in two sections at the number 7 hatch, the point of collision. The forward part is at about a 15-20 degree angle off the horizontal while the aft section is deck down at a 45 degree angle. Salvage operators examined the wreck but considered her unsalvageable. U.S. Steel, the parent company of the Bradley fleet, hired commercial divers to survey the wreck as well as recover any bodies still aboard, In three days of work, the remains

The Coast Guard icebreaker Mackinaw (shown in the newer red hull with Coast Guard slash) arrived on scene following the disaster. U.S. Coast Guard

of five men still trapped in the *Cedarville* were recovered. The loss of the ship was estimated at $3,500,000 with the cargo $21,000 additional.[xii]

The 603-foot, 8,575 gross registered ton *Cedarville* was built by the Great Lakes Engineering Works in 1927 at River Rouge, Michigan as the *A. F. Harvey*. In 1956 she was transferred from the U.S. Steel fleet to the Bradley fleet and sent to the Defoe Shipbuilding Company in Bay City, Michigan for conversion to a self-unloader. Bradley need more capacity to service the growing market for stone and the parent company provided it in the form of the *Harvey*. In the yard the ballast tanks were cut down, hoppers added in the holds and two 48-inch rubber conveyor belts installed. The conveyor fed a bucket elevator up to the 250-foot long unloading boom which in turn deposited the stone on the dock. Meanwhile the aft and forward houses were added to improve crew accommodations. When she came out of the yard she carried the name *Cedarville* in recognition of one of the fleet's frequent ports of call. Like the ill-fated *Carl D. Bradley*, she was a self-unloader working the limestone trade. With a 2,200 horsepower steam engine, she was underpowered compared to the Norwegian vessel, but this was typical for a laker. Martin E. Joppich of Rogers City, a veteran Great Lakes master was her captain.

History does repeat itself. Just a year after launching, the *Harvey* was involved in serious collision with the steamer *John Ericsson* on Lake Huron in a dense fog. The *Ericsson* was badly injured but the *Harvey* only slightly damaged. Now the roles were reversed.[xiii]

The Coast Guard Marine Board of Investigation immediately went to work to determine the cause of the

The Cedarville was built as the A.F. Harvey in 1927. Stonehouse Collection

disaster and what remedial actions were appropriate. It was a contentious investigation. Initially Captain Rasmus Haaland of the *Topdalsfjord* didn't appear since he was suffering from exhaustion and insomnia since the disaster. When he finally was questioned he claimed he saw the *Cedarville* turn 90 degrees in front of him and she was running too fast for conditions. Captain Joppich was also suffering from nervous exhaustion and he also appeared later in the hearings. He claimed according to the logged times and locations, the Norwegian ship was running too fast, averaging 6.5 mph from the bridge to the point of impact. Clearly she couldn't have been running as slow as Haaland claimed or the numbers would have proved the slower speed regardless of his contention. In the end, though Joppich was left "holding the bag." Some observers felt he took a bum rap.[xiv]

When it came to the conflicting testimony between the wheelsman and Captain Joppich, the Board believed the former and not the latter. They considered the Captain's recollection to be "self-serving and false." It didn't help matters that when divers recovered the logbook from the pilothouse it supported the wheelsman's testimony.[xv] They concluded the vessel ran at full speed from the time she left Calcite until just before the collision. The speed averaged from the Cheboygan Traffic Buoy to the impact with the *Topdalsfjord* equaled the nearly maximum speed of the ship loaded. Regardless of the reduced visibility in the fog she never slowed down. When she finally took evasive maneuvers as the unknown vessel approached she had considerable momentum and could not slow quickly. As the collision pattern was developing the captain should have slowed much earlier. Hindsight is remarkably clear![xvi]

When the captain was in doubt of the intention of the downbound vessel, Great Lakes Rule 26 called for him to reduce to bare steerageway or as was necessary in this instance, stop and reverse when within a half-mile radar range of the other vessel.[xvii] Joppich did not do so.

The Board concluded the *Topdalsfjord* was navigated with reasonable caution under the circumstances. At the time of the collision she was practically stopped. Even though the ship kept her course of 108 degrees past the normal turning point for entry to the South Channel, the Coast Guard felt it was prudent under the circumstances.

The Coast Guard also didn't approve of the *Cedarville's* efforts to beach herself. The Board felt the captain was certainly aware that the damage was serious enough to sink the ship quickly and he should have headed directly for the nearest shallow water, not taken the third mates course, which was in error. It was tragic that had he made for the nearest shallows, he had time to beach her, instead of trying to go twice as far for no good purpose.

There was no apparent reason for failure to establish radio communications between the *Topdalsfjord* and *Cedarville*, although it was possible three factors may have contributed to the problem. There were electrical disturbances which could have interfered with communications on channel 51. This was an old AM system and prone to such interference. The traffic between the *Topdalsfjord* and *Weissenberg* could have monopolized the channel preventing *Cedarville* calls from getting through. Of course the late recognition by the *Cedarville* that another vessel was running ahead of the German left little time for communication.[xviii]

The Board concluded the *Weissenberg's* rescue efforts were made with, "dispatch and efficiency in the best traditions of the sea." The surviving crew of the *Cedarville* owe their lives to the German sailors.

An unfortunate false belief that they could get the *Cedarville* to shallow water prevented the men from fully preparing to abandon her, or even bring all men on deck and out of confined spaces like the engine room. No abandon ship order was ever given.

It is worth noting that the decision to abandon ship is likely the most difficult a captain will make. The desire to stay with her is usually proven out by history as opposed to a hasty decision to dash for the boats at the first sign of trouble. It is a decision that if wrongly made or delayed, the master will be condemned most severely, as evidenced by the Coast Guard investigation.

When the Commandant of the Coast Guard reviewed the report he issued a conclusion stating, "The cause of the casualty was the failure of the master of the *SS Cedarville* to navigate his vessel in a period of reduced visibility in compliance with the Statutory Rules of the Road." Action was initiated to revoke his license. Captain Joppich did lose his ticket for a year and never sailed again. It is fair to say the *Cedarville* loss broke him.

On June 14, 1965 U.S. Steel abandoned all rights, title and interest in the wreck and so notified the Coast Guard and Army Corps of Engineers. Since it constituted a menace to navigation, the company recommended it be demolished with explosives as soon as possible.

Eventually U.S. Steel settled with the families of the ten dead crewmen and those injured for $2,400,000. It was a very expensive shipwreck. Considering the value of the vessel, $3,500,000, it was a loss of $6,000,000. Nine of the dead were from Rogers City. As with the *Carl D. Bradley* wreck seven years prior, it was a terrible blow to a small and tight knit community. Many of the Cedarville men and their families knew those on the *Bradley*. For Rogers City, shipwreck isn't something abstract, just a story in a newspaper or on a TV evening news report. It is very personal.

In 1966 the 620-foot *George A. Sloan* was transferred from U.S. Steel to the Bradley fleet to replace the *Cedarville*. After conversion to a self-unloader she retained her name.

In recognition of the actions of the *Weissenberg*, the Secretary of the Treasury awarded a "Gallant Ship Citation" to her and a plaque and ribbon bars to each participating crewmen.

The wreck of the *Cedarville* has become a popular although deadly attraction for scuba divers. The wreck is generally intact and it is possible to penetrate the interior. For the experienced wreck diver penetrating a wreck is safe. For the untrained and inexperienced, it can be deadly, especially a wreck like the *Cedarville* with a veil of piping, railing, wires and other assorted hazards hanging over her. At least one such diver was trapped inside. Only pure luck allowed his rescue. The first diving death was in 1965 when a young man tried to salvage the nameboard. Another diver died by a reported heart attack.[xix] In August 2003 a diver died while using a rebreather. While the wreck is in 102 feet of water, cabins and superstructure are reached at between 35-80 feet. She can be a very attractive wreck for inexperienced divers.[xx]

The *Cedarville* isn't forgotten. A recent book tries to lay the blame for the wreck squarely at the feet of U.S. Steel, that the company had a policy of not properly maintaining ships and demanding maximum season load totals from its captains which fostered a culture of excess speed, ultimately culminating in the *Cedarville* sinking. In my opinion this is so much balderdash. No company, big or small, can operate without maintaining its ships to a standard acceptable to the Coast Guard (which inspects them annually) and the underwriters. Certainly delivering the most cargo possible to meet customer demands is part of any shipping business, coal, iron ore, limestone or anything else. Nothing can be perfect and certainly risk is part of our daily lives, more so in maritime occupations simply by the nature of the trade. Ships don't earn their keep by moving at anything less than the most efficient speed. Time is money. A good radar and a trained and efficient pilothouse crew coupled with everyone following the rules (stated and implied), which in this instance meant maintaining a proper radio watch, is sufficient to keep shipping safe. But nothing is absolute.

Footnotes

[i]Marine Board of Investigation, convened to investigate the collision of the *SS Cedarville* and Norwegian *MV Topdalsfjord* on 7 May 1965 in the Straits of Mackinac with Loss of Life.

[ii]Marine Board.

[iii]Interview, Ric Mixter videotape, with Leonard Gabrysiak.

[iv]Marine Board.

[v]Marine Board.

[vi]Marine Board.

[vii]Marine Board.

[viii]Interview, Gabrysiak.

[ix]Interview, Gabrysiak.

[x]One survivor remembers it was a good shot of rum!

[xi]Maine Board.

[xii]Marine Board.

[xiii]Rev. Peter J. Van der Linden, editor, *Great Lakes Ships We Remember, Volume I,* (Cleveland: Freshwater Press, 1979), p. 75.

[xiv]Gerald F. Micketti, *The Bradley Boats*, (Traverse City, Michigan: Gerald F. Micketti, nd), pp. 35-42.

[xv]Interview, Gabrysiak.

[xvi]Marine Board.

[xvii]33 USC 291.

[xviii]Marine Board.

[xix]*Great Lakes Log*, June 26, 1995.

[xx]http://www.msue.msu.edu/isosco/cedarville.

ABOUT THE AUTHOR

Frederick Stonehouse holds a Master of Arts Degree in History from Northern Michigan University, Marquette, Michigan, and has authored many books on Great Lakes maritime history. *The Wreck Of The Edmund Fitzgerald, Lake Superior's "Shipwreck Coast," Dangerous Coast: Pictured Rocks Shipwrecks, Great Lakes Crime, Murder, Mayhem, Booze & Broads, Great Lakes Lighthouse Tales, Women And The Lakes, Untold Great Lakes Maritime Tales, Women And The Lakes II, More Untold Great Lakes Maritime Tales, Final Passage, True Shipwreck Adventures, My Summer At The Lighthouse, A Boy's Journal* and *Cooking Lighthouse Style, Favorite Recipes From Coast To Coast* are all published by Avery Color Studios, Inc.

He has been a consultant for both the U.S. National Park Service and Parks Canada, and an "on air" expert for National Geographic Explorer and the History Channel as well as many regional media productions. He has also taught Great Lakes Maritime History at Northern Michigan University and is an active consultant for numerous Great Lakes oriented projects and programs. Check frederickstonehouse.com for more details.

His articles have been published in *Skin Diver, Great Lakes Cruiser Magazine* and *Lake Superior Magazine*. He is a member of numerous boards of directors, including the Marquette Maritime Museum, U.S. Life-Saving Service Heritage Association, Northern Michigan University DeVos Art Museum.

Stonehouse resides in Marquette, Michigan.

**Other Frederick Stonehouse titles
by Avery Color Studios, Inc.**

- *Pirates, Crooks & Killers, The Dark
  Side Of The Great Lakes*
- *Blood On The Water, The Great Lakes
  During The Civil War*
- *November: The Cruelest Month,
  Great Lakes Wrecks*
- *The Wreck of the Edmund Fitzgerald,
  40th Anniversary Edition*
- *Great Lakes Crime
  Murder, Mayhem, Booze & Broads*
- *Women And The Lakes
  Untold Great Lakes Maritime Tales*
- *Went Missing Redux*
- *Final Passage, True Shipwreck Adventures*
- *My Summer At The Lighthouse, A Boys
  Journal*

Avery Color Studios, Inc. has a full line of Great Lakes
oriented books, cookbooks, shipwreck and lighthouse
maps, posters, stickers and magnets.

For a free full-color catalog, call:
1-800-722-9925
or visit us at: **averycolorstudios.com**

Avery Color Studios, Inc. products are available at gift
shops and bookstores throughout the Great Lakes region.